the 13th configuration

a memoir by Diane Lyoness

Diane Lyoness

The 13th Configuration

tellwell

Tellwell Talent
www.tellwell.ca

ISBN
978-1-77370-162-2 (Hardcover)
978-1-77370-161-5 (Paperback)
978-1-77370-163-9 (eBook)

Table of Contents

PART II

PART III

PART IV

Dedication

To my mother, who inspired me to be a kind and grateful human being, as she was.

To my daughter, Tina, and my son, Adam: I am not proud of some of the things I've done in the past, but I am so proud of both of you, and I am proud of who I am today.

To my husband, John: thank you for loving me and being my hero.

To my friend, Tricia, who convinced me to put my stories down on paper.

To my niece. Niki, a brilliant, beautiful and supportive young woman.

Preface

How different the world is today compared to the 20th Century, before there were cell phones or seat belts. Technology has made the earth seem smaller, yet there is more information available than we can handle. There are more choices and less self-control. In the 21st Century there is a spotlight on mental health, bullying, anxiety and teen suicide. This is serious. I believe raising entitled children in the last two decades has crippled them. How can we expect our kids to develop coping skills if they have never been challenged? How can they learn self-control if they have never been denied? They need less organization and more freedom to learn from their mistakes.

I grew up in a very different world. It was simpler and in some ways better. Children had no choices to deal with. They were to be seen and not heard, and often not even seen. At times it was cruel. But I learned to deal with it and I learned that happiness doesn't come from what you get… but from what you give.

Looking back, my life has been a whirlwind of extremes — extreme good and extreme bad — never ordinary. I wonder how much of it we cause for ourselves and how much is pre-determined by God's plan. The most traumatic event for me was June 11, 1966 — curiously 6/66 — just days before my 13th birthday. It was the day I discovered Heaven was real.

I started writing this book to tell the story of the traumatic struggles I endured and the reconfigurations that followed them. It wasn't until I finished the manuscript that I realized those events developed a sense of kindness, gratitude and resilience in me.

Reading my story may bring gratitude to those who have stability in their lives and, I hope, comfort to those who don't. We have to take responsibility for our choices, but that doesn't mean we will have control over our lives. Everything happens for a reason. I have learned to accept what I cannot change. I find both solace and humour in the following quote:

"If you want to make God laugh, tell Him your plans for the future."

PART I

Chapter 1

Where it all Started

On average I have had a life-changing event every three years over the last 60 years, some good and some bad. The first 20 years were the most traumatic and the next 40 were the most extreme.

I was born Diane Edith McKone on June 30, 1953, the last day of the first half of the year, and the day before Canada's birthday. There was a little light rain that day, according to the records. My mother, Patricia McKone, née Roth, brought me home to the Roth family farm northeast of Stratford, Ontario, to live with her mother Edith and her father Mervin.

My father, Allan McKone, lived one concession away on his parents' farm. They were married before I was born but he moved out when I was a few months old. I never knew why he didn't live with us. Mom only said that he always thought he was right. Apparently, he used to say, "If I was wrong I would admit it, but so far in my life I have never been wrong." Decades later, when I was an adult and my mother had passed away, her youngest sister, Aunt Rene, told me that my parents may have had a chance at marriage if they hadn't lived with the in-laws. But as it was, I lived the first eight years of my life with Mom, Grandma, Grandpa, and the occasional relative or border. We lived in a large century farmhouse with lots of activity, lots of good times, and lots of drinking, cursing, and fighting.

My oldest memory was the day of my 1st birthday party. Some people say you can't remember back that far but my memory is vivid. I was standing by the kitchen table. It was higher than my eye level. I caught sight of coloured balloons on top of the table, but in the background was the sound of children screaming. I felt confused. That's the extent of the memory. Apparently, Mom invited a few toddlers of her friends and they were not in a party mood. I was not used to being around other children. I think we were all scared. I wasn't crying... just observing.

The first five years before I started school were full of wonder on the farm. As an only child I had three make believe friends: Toby, Keebee and Gaw. They were either boys or sexless, I can't say for sure. I just know they were like souls that were there with me. I talked to them. I referred to them often when talking to Mom.

"What are you doing?" she asked one day.

"Playing with Keebee," I replied.

"Who is Keebee?"

"Keebee's Keebee."

"Where does Keebee live?" she asked.

"Keebee lives in Keebee's house!" I retorted.

It must have been frustrating for her and I did not know how to explain them. Near the end of our imaginary friendship, I remember being in the bathroom and Toby was sitting on the toilet. Mom came in and I shouted "Don't sit there! Toby's there."

She jokingly said, "I'm going to flush him down," and with that she flushed the toilet. I was horrified and broke into a huge wail. She immediately tried to console me, saying "No I didn't! No I didn't! See... he's still there." It seems weird that I remember thinking, "Does she really see him? Is she lying to me? Can I trust her?" I don't remember whether my friends ever came back after that. What do you suppose it means?

I created playmates because I was alone. I had a large playroom with lots of toys and a gigantic imagination. The farm, the barn, the pump house, the shed, and the rusty equipment burial yard in the tall grass behind the drive shed... they were all ripe for imagination.

My world expanded when my older cousins came to visit. We walked down to the creek and looked for little people hiding under the rocks. Yes,

I fell for that. They kept seeing them and I kept missing them. I wanted so badly to find one.

I learned that you can't climb on top of the car and slide down it without your mom knowing, because the paint colour is on the back of your pants. It was a white 1956 Chevrolet with a green roof. My little cousin, Billy, and I thought it would make a fun slide, but we were careful that no one was watching.

"What were you doing?" Mom asked later.

"Playing behind the shed."

"Were you in the shed near the car?"

"No."

"Were you in the car?"

"No."

"Were you anywhere near the car?"

"No."

"Are you sure you didn't touch the car?"

"Yes, we're sure."

"What's that on the back of your pants?"

Our bottoms were the same green colour as the roof of the car. There were other telltale signs on the car as well. It became clear to me that although I had done a bad thing, lying about it was even worse. That lesson stuck with me. Never lie to Mom because you will always get caught. I don't remember ever lying to her again. My face would betray me.

I learned what a four-year-old boy's private parts look like from watching Billy urinate behind the drive-shed, and I felt naughty. But I was still curious.

We celebrated major family events like Christmas and birthdays at our farm because it was spacious. Those were the social times with laughter, games and cousins of all ages. Mom was the seventh of nine live births that Grandma Roth endured. Mom's siblings had all married and left the nest, except for my Uncle Bob. He was dropped on his head when he was a baby and didn't learn to speak until he was nine years old. He lived on the farm with us but I don't remember him being present much of the time. He must have been about 26 when I was born and therefore maybe worked somewhere. He seemed normal to me; he was nice and I liked him.

So, these family reunions were invigorating. Cousins were running and playing all over the house. I was the second youngest and tried to keep up to the eight- to twelve-year-olds. We always played Hide-and-Seek.

In the 1950s those old farmhouses had coal-fired furnaces with stove pipes running up through the floors to heat the rooms. When I was about three, the furnace was converted to oil-forced air and the stove pipes were removed. So why did they not properly cover the hole in the living room floor where the round stove pipe had been? It was in a corner and a big comfy chair was placed in front of it. I hid behind the chair and fell through the hole and landed in the retired coal bin in the basement. No one could find me. What a great hiding place! A desperate search and the sounds of a whimpering child led the adults to me. I was traumatized and black with soot. And then a year or so later, another reunion, another game, and I did the same stupid thing again. This time the coal bin was gone, the storm windows were in the basement propped up against the wall, and I fell through four panes of glass. Not a scratch on me. But again, no one could find me until someone remembered the hole. I was trapped under the window frames, with glass shards all around me, crying and scared. I heard feet running back and forth on the hardwood floors above me. It seemed like a long time before they found me.

Most of my memories of life on the farm were so fond and sacred that when we moved to the city I so missed it that I dreamed about it for years. Even as an adult I would wake up with tears in my eyes and a heavy heart. But there were also traumatic events that shaped my personality in a negative way.

Chapter 2

Too Young to Cope

Grandpa was the best. I would follow him to the barn and tailgate him all around the farm. He was tall and lanky but he always bent over to talk to me; he never talked down to me. Grandma made delicious pies but there was only one piece for each person. I would eat mine and let Grandpa know that if he didn't want his I would eat it for him. He would hand it to me saying he was full. Mom soon put a stop to that con. The point is that I loved, and was loved by, all the adults in the house. I was very fortunate.

What I didn't know was that Mom felt we had to stay living on the farm so she could keep an eye on Grandma when Grandpa came home drunk. Grandpa worked at the CNR shops. They performed maintenance for the Canadian National Railway in Stratford. He also tended to the cows and pigs on the farm. Mom worked in the city at various factories, stores and restaurants. Grandma looked after me and we tended to the gardens and the chickens. But Grandma and Grandpa didn't seem to like each other very much, and Mom was caught in the middle. Often the fights escalated to a dangerous point. Yelling, swearing, name-calling, fists raised on the verge of violence. I loved them all, but it was too much to bear. I ran from the conflict and sat on the back stairs with my fingers clenched in my hair. Curled up in a ball and rocking gently I would drift off to another place. Mom found me and had a difficult time trying to untangle my fingers from my hair. I couldn't speak. I was numb. To this day I avoid conflict of any kind whenever possible. I believe this was the first of many events that moulded me into a people-pleaser. I can adapt like a chameleon to any situation to avoid conflict. In the process, I lost a part of my identity.

Mom was 21 when I was born and within a few months she found herself single. While I was still small enough to sit on Grandma's lap, but old enough to sense tension, I remember times when Mom wanted to go out in the evening with friends. Grandma thought that was wrong and that people would talk. By the serious accusations from Grandma I was worried for Mom and cried for her to stay home.

Grandma held me and said, "Now look what you've done."

Grandpa pointed his long, crooked finger down the road and yelled, "You should be down there with him."

"Never mind I'll stay home for the rest of my life," ranted Mom, throwing down her purse and her coat.

It scared me when Mom acted like that. I stopped crying and indicated I was alright with her going out. After she left, Grandma rocked me and gently ran her fingers along my arms. Then everything was quiet and I went to sleep believing Mom would be back, and she always came back.

After dinners, Grandpa would go to his room, lie on his bed and read the paper. Grandma had a separate bedroom. I liked to lie next to Grandpa and talk to him while he read. I'd ramble on about my day with Toby and Keebee or sing nursery rhymes. He pretended to listen. I liked the smell of his pipe tobacco. It reminded me of apples and cinnamon in the winter. Mom would check in often until it was time for me to go to my room. I sensed she didn't like that I was with Grandpa. When I pressed her with "Why?" she told me that one time he tried to suffocate her with a pillow and then he apologized. He thought she was Grandma. I thought about that and decided Grandpa wasn't a danger to me.

My most vivid traumatic memories are around the age of four. As I said, I loved when family came to the farm. This time it was a summer picnic in the front yard. My cousins were playing on the swings. The women were in the house gabbing and cleaning up after dinner. The uncles were lined up in chairs along the tree-lined yard watching the children play. Uncle Red was married to Mom's older sister, Aunt Eunice. Their daughter, Judy, was about 10 and we were swinging together. Uncle Red called me over to him.

"No, don't go. Stay here," Judy said.

He called again and she cautioned me again. I didn't know what to do. I hesitated.

"Come on now. Be a good girl," Uncle Red said.

As I walked toward him I sensed everyone was looking at me. When I reached him he yanked my pants down! Then all the men laughed. I was so embarrassed that I couldn't even reach down to pull up my pants. Instead, I waddled with my pants around my ankles, crying, across the lawn, towards the house. Hearing the commotion, the ladies came out on the porch.

Aunt Eunice disgustingly called "Red... what did you do?"

"I don't care what he thinks of me," my mother said angrily, "but he doesn't have to take it out on my child!"

She pulled my pants up and took me into the house. I remember feeling stunned. At that tender age all I could think was, "What did she mean? What does he think of my mom? Why did he pick on me? Why did I deserve that? What was wrong with Mom and me?" I felt broken. I felt less than. I never trusted Uncle Red again. He was my only uncle that I couldn't trust.

Another time he told me to watch him blow smoke out his eyes. He inhaled smoke from a cigarette, and while I closely watched his eyes, he burnt my arm with the cigarette. I jumped. He laughed. I felt so sorry for his daughter and his son. They had a nasty father.

Chapter 3

Father Figures

I had some wonderful father figures in my life, but I have no memories of seeing my father at my home. He lived with his mother and father just a mile down the road at the McKone farm. Mom said she used to take me to visit there but I only remember visiting Grandma and Grandpa McKone a couple of times. As an adult, I reconnected with my Grandma McKone and her daughter, Aunt Lois. Both were very kind and loving ladies.

Mom had two brothers. Uncle Bob, as I said, was older but mentally only an adolescent. I could relate to him. He was a kind man. Uncle Bill was a year younger than Mom and he was a handsome, shy, proper gentleman. I was his flower girl when he married, and he walked me down the aisle the first time I was married. He died from cancer in 1997, the year after Mom died from cancer.

Uncle Art was married to Mom's sister, Aunt Rene. He was a very special man. He nicknamed me DEMI from my initials. He was jolly, always smiling, and like a brother to Mom. I often went on summer vacations with Uncle Art and Aunt Rene in their trailer. I stayed with them when I was nine and Mom was on her honeymoon for her second marriage.

Uncle Bud was married to Mom's older sister, Aunt Dolly. Every summer Grandma Roth and I took the train from Stratford to Ottawa or wherever my uncle was stationed with the Ontario Provincial Police. Uncle Bud was funny and I felt safe with him. He would set me on his lap in a big flowered armchair and read me stories until I fell asleep. After many years of trying, they finally had a daughter, born when I was five, and we continued to visit them every summer. I finally had a younger girl cousin to spend vacations with. We would go shopping, to exhibitions, to beaches, and many times to the Parliament buildings in Ottawa. Uncle Bill, Uncle Art and Uncle Bud filled the void left by my father walking away from us.

Chapter 4

Twelve Schools in Thirteen Years

At age five I started school in the city. The country school was about a three mile walk and I had no one to walk with. So, Mom arranged for me to attend Juliet School in the city, and dropped me off in the mornings at Aunt Eunice and Uncle Red's house. I walked to school and returned there for the afternoons until she picked me up after work. On one of my early days in kindergarten my father, Allan McKone, entered my classroom. He was a teacher at that school and Mom mentioned that I may see him. I waved and said, "Hi Allan." I was quite proud that I knew him personally. He nodded to me. When I got home that evening Mom sat me down and explained that I shouldn't have done that. I must call him Mr. McKone at school. I was hurt. He felt that I had been rude. I didn't understand that it was a matter of respect and I don't remember seeing him there again. Maybe I didn't want to see him. Maybe he didn't want his colleagues to know that he had a child.

I was shy and thus observed how other kids interacted. There was a play kitchen set up in a secluded corner of the classroom. One day I was in there alone when a quiet boy joined me and cooperatively pretended to be heating the kettle and operating the toaster with me. We played without saying a word. I never saw him again. Thirty years later I discovered what happened that day. His name was John and he was only four. His brother, Ron, was five and in my kindergarten class. They looked alike. Ron didn't like school, so one day he stayed home and John went to school for him. Their mother told me the teacher didn't know the difference. They could have pulled it off if John hadn't come home announcing, "Look what I made in school." His mom promptly moved Ron from the morning class to the afternoon class, when John was having his nap. John must have been the boy that I met once in the kitchen and never saw again for three decades.

During that kindergarten year, I met two girls in my class that I became friends with. The first girl lived next door to Aunt Eunice. I don't remember her name. We walked to school together and played in the afternoons.

I told her wonderful stories of how I lived on a farm that had a circus and rides, and I embellished the fantasy such that I began to believe it myself. She wanted to go there. I knew the way to the country farm from driving with Mom.

So, I said, "Sure let's go." We set out after lunch walking down the main street of Stratford, towards the outskirts of the city. The fact that there would be no circus when we got there never occurred to me. It seemed like an adventure. We never got there. Another of Mom's sisters, Aunt Marie, happened to drive by and saw us walking down the highway. She stopped, made us get in the car and took my friend back home. I knew I was in trouble but I don't recall the details. I just remember that the other girl was promptly switched to the afternoon class and Aunt Eunice was not pleased that I took off while she was watching her soap operas. That's likely why I don't remember the name of the girl next door. I never saw her again.

Needless to say, at the end of kindergarten my Aunt Eunice ended the contract, so Mom had to search for a new sitter. Uncle Art had a sister, Gertie, who had three children my age and she agreed to have me there. So, I was enrolled in Grade 1 at Romeo School. On the first day, I was dropped off at the new school with my kindergarten report card in hand. While sitting on the gym floor waiting for my name to be called, the boy next to me asked why I had a picture on my report card envelope.

"My kindergarten teacher put it there," I said.

"You're lying," he said. "You're going to get in trouble for that."

That scared me. I knew I didn't do it, but this was a different school. I had no idea what they would do to me and I didn't know anyone else there. This was my first re-configuration experiment. I became acutely aware of every move around me, copying their actions and expressions so as to blend in with my environment.

For whatever reason, I was only at Gertie's for half of Grade 1. I must have done something wrong again. In the winter, Mom moved me back to Juliet School. Remember I mentioned a second friend in kindergarten? Her name was Beth and her mom became my new sitter. Beth had two younger sisters and a brother. I liked being at her house because I could get lost in the commotion and her mom was so nice. But that only lasted until the end of Grade 1.

When I was seven, my godmother (Mom's sister Aunt Beatrice) fell sick with cancer. She was in her mid-thirties, with a husband who was in the army stationed in Egypt, and three sons at home. She was a saint of a lady. Only the good die young. When she fell sick her youngest son, Billy, came to live at our farm. So, he and I walked the long road to the country school together. It was a one-room school for Grades 1 to 8. He was in Grade 1 and I was in Grade 2. We were like brother and sister and, at times, I felt a little jealous sharing my mom with him.

Aunt Beatrice came home from the hospital to live with us for her final days, and when the end came, Billy and I stood at the screen door watching the ambulance take her away. That is another vivid memory. Our fingers and foreheads were pressed tightly against the wire screen.

Billy softly spoke what I was thinking: "My mom's not coming back..."

I remember that moment so clearly. My heart ached for him. After the funeral Billy went to live with his dad. I seldom saw him after that because they moved far away. Many years later, at my grandma's 80th birthday, we would reconnect.

At that one-room school in the country only four students were in Grade 2: three farm boys and me. I was shy and they didn't talk to girls. Our desks were at the back of the room near the door to the stairs. One day when the lunch bell rang I moved towards the door and a mob of hungry kids pushed their way down the stairs to the lunchroom in the basement. I got caught in the middle and tumbled into a ball on the cement, spraining my ankle. By the end of the day my foot was the size of a football and the teacher gave me a ride home. That was my last day at that school.

Mom worked in the office of a meatpacking plant. She found a lunchtime sitter near her work and I finished Grade 2 at Hamlet School. There I found a friend in Betty-Ann, and I learned a new emotion: empathy. I felt sad for Betty-Ann. She had tatted hair, ragged clothes and no mother to comfort her.

We were seven years old and inseparable at school. She lived with her father and brother in a shack of a house with no refrigerator. They had a cow out back and the milk was kept in a galvanized pail on the floor in the kitchen. It had dead flies floating on top. I politely refused when offered a drink. It was winter and outside her house was a six-foot hill covered in snow that we loved to climb and slide down. That is, until Mom picked me up and noticed the back of my snowsuit was covered in manure. The hill was a manure pile. That was the end of going to Betty-Ann's house to play.

I still had lunch at the sitter's house, but after school I walked to the meat-packing plant and sat in Mom's office until quitting time. It was fascinating. Her co-workers were very nice, and I was allowed to use the adding machine and pretend I worked there. Outside the building I could see the cows riding up the ramp to the slaughter house, oblivious to where they were going. On occasion I had a tour of the cold room where the carcasses were hung on big scary meat hooks. I could handle that because I had seen my grandfather cut the heads off chickens, and one ran around the barn headless. I saw a mother pig bite the throat and take the life of our collie dog, Laddy, when she thought he was too close to her piglets. I learned to be cautious.

About this time, Mom met a nice man named Ralph. On weekends he took us to the beach and to places kids love, like Storybook Gardens. He had a delightful English accent. He gave me an electric organ and I learned to play Christmas carols.

At the end of Grade 2 it was my 8th birthday and I learned that Grandma was selling the farm. Mom rented a two-bedroom basement apartment in a house on Douglas Street in Stratford. I had to give away my boxer dog that I'd had for six years. Although I was extremely sad I knew there was nothing to be gained in begging or whining. The decision was made.

Grandma moved in with us. Mom and I shared a bedroom as we had since I was born. I was excited about moving to the city but I had no idea I would miss life on the farm as much as I did in the years to come. I missed

Grandpa. He apparently was put in a boarding house and I only saw him twice before he died a year or so later.

That summer Grandma went to visit her daughter in Seattle without me. At the age of eight, I was considered mature enough to stay by myself while Mom was at work. Mrs. Schrader lived upstairs and I could go to her if I needed anything. A lunch was left in the fridge for me. Curiously, I spent much of the day listening to adult music on our phonograph and learning the songs. I learned the words to every hymn on the album "Sing Along with Tennessee Ernie Ford." I loved to sing but I'm told I can't carry a tune. I loved music. When I was very small, Mom carried me in her arms and danced to country music and we sang the words together. My favourites were "It is no Secret", "Open up Your Heart", "Lonely Little Robin", and, of course, "You are my Sunshine." Mom had a beautiful voice.

Like country mouse to city mouse I had a new home, a new school, a new configuration of sorts. I made a new friend, Janice, who lived on my street and we went to Avon school together in Grade 3. It was great to belong to the same bunch of friends for a whole year. There was also Joan, Gary, John, Wendy, Gail and Margaret. I had a real social network. Mom was still seeing Ralph, but I felt tension around him when other family members were present. My uncles were not fond of him, but no one would tell me why. Adults would whisper about him around me. Then, on my 9th birthday Mom and Ralph were married. My life took another drastic change.

Chapter 5

The 2nd Configuration: My New Father

That summer, after Grade 3, I went on a number of vacations with various relatives. When I returned to Stratford, my friends greeted me with an exciting new game. At the end of our street was a five acre field of tall grass. In the middle they had flattened a spot where we could sit down, play spin-the-bottle and smoke cigarettes. It was naughty and it was fun. We always shared one cigarette at a time and passed it around. In order to get the 25 cents to buy a pack, we bought a cake for less money, and sold tickets door-to-door to raffle it off. That worked about twice before no one in the neighbourhood wanted to buy more raffle tickets. After that summer, I would not smoke again until I was 16 and back in Stratford.

Playing spin-the-bottle meant kissing a boy for the first time. Even with lips clenched it was not very pleasant. I soon learned to attempt to direct the spin. There was one boy who I didn't mind kissing, but I wasn't prepared for what came next. Although we thought our hiding place was secret, we had been found out by my new step-father.

When they married, Ralph moved into my Mom's bedroom and I moved into Grandma's room. In the evenings after dinner we watched TV in a very tiny living room. I loved having a father and sitting on his knee with his comforting arms around me. It felt nice when he tenderly tickled my arm as Grandma used to do when I was small enough to sit on her lap. When no one else was present he began to run his fingers down my leg. This too felt nice and comforting. Then his fingers wandered to places I didn't like. I froze! I was embarrassed and didn't know what to do. I was afraid that if I moved it would be too obvious and I wanted to believe it wasn't happening. I worked up the nerve to yawn, slide off his lap, and go to bed.

Not willing to give up on my new father, and not understanding what had happened, I continued to sit on his lap. Maybe this was a normal thing. How would I know what fathers do? I never had a real one before. He continued the pattern and I continued to shy away. One time he actually tried to insert his finger in my vagina. That was unbearable! When Mom and I were alone I summoned the courage to tell her what he did, and that I didn't like it, and would she please tell him to stop. She was shocked and said she would talk to him. I wasn't sure if she believed me. Later she took me aside and told me his response. He said he was trying to discover what we children were doing in our hide-away in the field. My mind exploded! My friends would never do anything like that. It was a big deal just to kiss. But Mom believed me now. She started to cry, saying she didn't know what to do. She had just married him and now this happens. I felt I may have ruined her life. I didn't know what I wanted her to do about it, but I just hoped she could make it all go away. She asked me if I wanted her to leave him. I couldn't tell her that, so I told her I would be OK. We made a pact that she wouldn't leave me alone with him, and I wouldn't sit on his lap anymore. Then I found out we were moving again. Mom and Ralph were buying a semi-detached house in London, Ontario. I was going to have to suck it up and put this behind me.

I started Grade 4 at Avon School in Stratford and two months later said a tearful good-bye to all my friends. I would finish Grade 4 at C.C. Carruthers School in London. It was a long walk from our subdivision in Glen Cairn Woods, across the busy Commissioners Road, and down Adelaide Street. While at that school, I had the opportunity to sing in a four-girl ensemble. We sang "Puff the Magic Dragon" on CFPL Television's *The Salty Show*. I was so excited to be on TV.

When I brought home my first report card it stated that my name was Diane Bailey. Mom's first remark was, "Your last name isn't Bailey."

"But your name is Bailey," I said. "I thought my name changed when your name changed."

We had never discussed this and I just assumed it. So, she called the school and explained that my last name was McKone. They understood and agreed that I could use the name Bailey informally with my friends as long as I used McKone on legal papers. I continued to use Bailey and when I was 16 and applied for a Social Insurance number, I forgot to use McKone. I received a letter indicating attempted fraud since Diane Edith Bailey did not exist. I was soon able to clear that up without too much trouble.

Our house in London had four bedrooms. Grandma Roth and Uncle Bob lived with us. It was here that I met Pam who turned out to be my longest-term BFF and my Maid of Honour at my first marriage.

We met when Pam and I signed up for violin lessons. I learned two songs — "Twinkle, Twinkle Little Star" and "Three Blind Mice" — and they both sounded the same when I practised. Within six months we both quit playing violin. Our parents were pleased, and from those lessons our parents also became best friends. That is why Pam and I were able to keep in touch over the years, in spite of our many moves to come.

In 1963, Glen Cairn School was built in our subdivision and Pam and I had a short walk to a new school for Grade 5. Lots of new homes were being built and we had great fun playing in them in their various stages of completion. Looking back now it was a little dangerous and very daring. But those days were generally safe for children of age 10 to roam the neighbourhood, hone their athletic skills, and only come home when they were hungry or it was dark.

One day, out of the blue, my birth father Allan called and said he wanted to come visit me. I was excited about the prospect that he wanted to see me. On the day he was to arrive Mom was at work and Grandma was drying dishes. She mumbled to me, "If I were you I would just tell him that 'First I had no fathers... now I don't need two fathers' and tell him he can leave." I didn't want to say that because it felt mean. But I did it. I felt I had to. It seems I always did what I was told to. Allan arrived with flowers and a book for me. He had red hair and freckles. I didn't recognize him, so it wasn't too hard to tell him that I didn't need two fathers. Many years later I regretted that. I never saw him again until my Grandfather McKone's funeral when I was a divorced mother with two young children.

That house in London is where I lived when President Kennedy died, John Glenn orbited the earth, the Beatles came to America, and my little sister was conceived. I was ecstatic at the thought of having a brother or sister. Unfortunately, it meant we had to move again for various reasons. Grandma didn't like Uncle Bob's room in the basement so the two of them moved back to Stratford. Mom, Dad and I moved to a two-bedroom apartment in London in the summer of 1964. Sadly, I had to give away my new dog again but, on the bright side, the apartment had a swimming pool and we were preparing for a new baby.

I started Grade 6 at Princess Elizabeth School, and Pam and I were still best friends and visited every weekend. My sister, Alison, was born October 1, 1964. I was both her big sister and her second mother. I could calm her when she was colicky even better than Mom could. Two months later Ralph started selling real estate on the side, and convinced Mom to move to a three-bedroom house in south London. After Christmas of 1964 my new school was Tecumseh for the remainder of Grades 6, 7 and 8. I thrived there with teachers, girlfriends, boyfriends, activities, and Pam remained my best friend.

The year 1966 started out great at Tecumseh school. In the winter, I won the Public Speaking Award for my speech about the joys and trials of an 18-month-old baby sister. In the spring, I enjoyed the lead role in a school play about a library and a bookworm. I played the naughty girl who needed to learn the value of books. Students were asking for my autograph. I had my first steady boyfriend of three months. I was at the top of my game, living in reality rather than my fantasy world, and taking ballet lessons. I aspired to be a dancer — and then the unthinkable happened.

Chapter 6

The Day that Changed My Life Forever

June 11, 1966 was a sunny Saturday and our family was going to the beach at Lake Erie. On the way, we were going to deliver my goldfish to a friend's fish pond. It was two weeks before my 13th birthday and the fish were not getting much attention anymore. My step-father was driving. Mom and my 20-month-old sister Alison were in the back seat. I was in the front passenger seat holding the goldfish. Our car had no seat belts so I lay down and curled up on the front seat for the hour-long drive.

As we neared St. Thomas we were looking for a particular side road where the fish pond was. Thinking we had passed it, we used a farmer's lane to turn around. A police car was sitting in the farmer's lane. We didn't know that he was waiting to catch a speeding car that was spotted by a police helicopter. As we turned around and headed back in the opposite direction we were moving at about 40 mph and approaching a hill in the road. A car flew over the hill, passing another car and hit us head-on. The police had clocked the speeder at 110 mph and since we were travelling at a speed of 40 mph, the collision had an impact of 150 mph or 241 km/h according to the police report. Both vehicles crushed like an accordion and the engines caught fire. Police were there in seconds because they were waiting for Tom Wildgust and his passenger friend who were drunk and joy-riding. The passenger was killed instantly and Tom had both legs broken.

I remember the split second before the spectacular crash. I was curled up on the front seat. Mom screamed and I looked up... then nothing. My memory recalls no crash, no noise, only silence. I must have blacked out. My next memory is sitting on the floor in the front passenger seat in a crouching position facing the passenger door. My left knee was ripped wide open to the bone. The flesh inside looked like cottage cheese and red Jello. I felt no pain. I was numb. I recall thinking that I needed a band aid. I heard Mom moan in the back seat and a brief glance revealed her face covered in blood. I didn't want to look at her. We later discovered that inertia threw her from the back seat through the front windshield, and brought her back again into the back seat. I was thrown into the dashboard and onto the floor. I could not see my step-father behind me, but I believe he was unconscious. My 20-month-old sister Alison was standing on the back seat screaming but unhurt. Thanks be to God! They say that small children and intoxicated people roll with the flow which helps to protect them.

I have no idea how long it was before a policeman lifted me out of the car and set me in the back seat of his cruiser with an unknown lady bystander who was holding my sister. This lady talked sweetly to me. She called me "Honey" and tried to keep me awake and talking. I tried, but failed, and I fell into oblivion.

Crashed car June 1966

Londoner dies, 4 hurt in three-car collision

PORT STANLEY—A London man was killed and five persons—four from one family—injured in a spectacular three - car crash about two miles north of here Saturday afternoon.

George Patrick McGregor, 40, of 528 Pall Mall, a passenger in one of the cars, died at the scene.

Driver of the car, Thomas George Wildgust, 24, of the same address, is in critical condition at St. Thomas-Elgin General Hospital with chest and head injuries and fractured legs.

Ralph Bailey, 35, of 214 Langley St., driver of another car, is in fair condition with arm and face cuts.

His wife Pat, 34, is in serious condition with a fractured wrist, face cuts and head injuries, while his 13-year-old daughter Dianne is in critical condition with a fractured thigh, chest and internal injuries.

The couple's 1½-year-old

GEORGE PATRICK McGREGOR

daughter Alison is in good condition with scrapes.

Police said the accident occurred when Mr. Wildgust's car overtook one driven by Samuel Kydd, of Hamilton.

The southbound Wildgust car struck the left rear of the Kydd vehicle and swerved head-on into the Bailey car. Mr. Kydd was not hurt.

Highway 4 traffic was detoured for more than an hour.

Mr. McGregor is survived by his wife, the former Doris Davis; mother, Mrs. William (Edna) McGregor, Chatham; daughters, Patricia, Edna Rose and Anita, all at home; sons, Edward and Michael, both at home; sister, Mother Mary Bridget, Windsor; and brothers, William, Point Edward and Gerald, Fraser, Mich.

Requiem Mass will be held 9 a.m. Wednesday in St. Agnes Church, Chatham. Burial is in St. Anthony's Cemetery, Chatham. T. Brady Hinnegan Funeral Home, Chatham, in charge.

St. Thomas news article regarding spectacular three-car crash

I had a long and powerful dream. I was flying in an open vehicle like a chariot or a magic carpet. I was with a tall figure in a long white robe. I sensed it was a man but I did not see a face. He was a good man. I was not afraid because I was where I wanted to be. I could see the earth moving farther and farther away, and I knew all was as it should be.

And then I woke up and I was sad. I was in a bed with a curtain drawn around it. I heard a lady talking to a man on the other side of that curtain.

She said to him, "So help me... if that little girl dies I will never forgive you." Those were the first words that I heard while trying to figure out where I was.

As it turns out I had been in the Intensive Care Unit of the St. Thomas General Hospital for about two weeks. Now that I was awake I would be moved to a semi-private room with my mom for the next month. I will never forget the moment they wheeled her bed into my room. Her entire head was bandaged like a zombie and her right arm was in a bent cast. As if that wasn't scary enough, when the doctor unwound all her bandages the prickly ends of more than 100 stitches were sticking out all over her face, with hardened bits of dried blood here and there. She asked me if she looked bad. I smiled and told her "not really." They would not let her have a mirror. I tried to cheer her up and make her laugh. In a few days, she was strong enough to slowly make her way to the bathroom. When she looked in the mirror she screamed and wept. There was nothing I could do. My left leg was tied to the ceiling in traction and I could not move. My heart went out to her. She looked like the walking dead.

That is where I spent my 13th birthday. I had a broken femur but was very fortunate that I did not lose my leg at the knee. It was sewn back together and I ended up with a huge, jagged scar. I was later told that my ribs were broken and one of them punctured my right lung. The lung collapsed and I died on the operating table for a few minutes before the surgeon re-inflated my lung and started my heart again with the hopes that the lung would remain inflated. That explains why the lady in ICU said what she said to her husband who was driving the car that hit us. It was many months later when I reflected on my injuries and the dream I'd had. I am convinced I had a glimpse of life after death. That was 50 years ago and ever since that event I have felt a bond with God and no fear of death. The following quote says it very well:

Perhaps it is easiest to understand this way...

"How does one become a butterfly?" she asked pensively.

***"You must want to fly so much that you are
willing to give up being a caterpillar."***

— TRINA PAULUS

While in the hospital I received birthday cards and letters from friends, teachers, family, and even people I hardly knew. My very first love letter came from my boyfriend, Paul, who wrote about the beautiful Grade 8 graduation he witnessed. He wrote that he couldn't wait until next year when we could dance together at our graduation. He signed it: "Love Paul."

I could not leave my bed because my left leg was tied up in traction due to my broken hip. When I was bored, I counted the holes in the squares of ceiling tiles to see if they all had the same number, and if the patterns were identical. I had a TV to watch. The handheld wired control box was also a sound speaker with tiny holes in the controller. One day I was absent-mindedly sticking a safety pin in and out of the holes when the pin pierced a wire. I immediately got a bolt of electricity that jolted my leg in traction and the TV began to smoke. Next the fire alarm rang out and commotion was everywhere. Fire trucks arrived. Patients were being wheeled out of their rooms. In half an hour everything was cleared and calmed down. I was so embarrassed.

As for my mother, she was released from hospital a couple of weeks before me. She continued to pull tiny shards of glass from her face for the next 30 years. Her right arm was broken in three places and she never again had full use of it. My step-father, who had been an architectural engineer, had his eye sewn back in its socket but never again had clear enough vision to produce fine drawings. He also suffered brain trauma and personality disorder which resulted in marriage breakdown and divorce within three years... more about that story later. Little Alison lived with my Aunt Eunice until Mom and Dad were home and able to take care of her.

Chapter 7

That Which Doesn't Kill You... Makes You Stronger

I came home from the hospital in August 1966 with a body cast from my left ankle to my left armpit. I could not bend at the waist to sit up, but I could stand with crutches if two people lifted me to a vertical position. My poor mother had a cast on her arm and a toddler to look after, not to mention the worries of no income for the family. Ralph was confused most of the time. So, life had to be simplified. We all lived on the first floor of our house and turned the dining room into a bedroom for Mom and Ralph. I slept on the living room couch. My long blonde hair was cut short to make it easier to wash and care for. The worst part was going to the bathroom with the body cast on. First Mom tried putting a bedpan under me on the couch. But the urine ran up my back under the cast. We soon discovered the only method that worked was for two people (Mom and Ralph) to stand me up. Then while Mom helped to balance me with her one arm, Ralph had to wedge a plastic pail between my legs just above the knees. Since the cast wrapped around my hips, my right leg could only spread to about hip width. I urinated in the pail. I was humiliated! I was 13 years old and beginning to grow pubic hair. The man who did that terrible thing that we didn't talk about anymore had to kneel in front of me, his face near my pelvis, and hold the pail for me to pee in. I tried to control my bladder release to twice a day to minimize this horrid routine. No words can explain how much I wanted to just disappear. Even now, writing about it makes me shake nervously.

My boyfriend, Paul, came and visited me once. I didn't know he was coming. I looked horrible in a body cast and housecoat and chopped off hair. I was uncomfortable because I had to pee and was holding it. We played board games. He was very polite, almost formal. He told me his family was moving. I never saw him again. That's how bad I looked.

The body cast was removed in September 1966. I started Grade 8 on crutches and continued therapy until my leg was strong enough to walk. But from the day the cast came off I could tell that my left leg was shorter than my right leg. My knees were not at the same level. I walked with a limp. The doctor thought that perhaps the left femur bone overlapped when it healed. So, in the spring of 1967 I went back in the hospital, the femur bone was re-broken and a steel pin was inserted down the centre of the bone to hold it in place. No cast this time, but I was on crutches, non-weight bearing, for the entire summer before high school. I missed my Grade 8 graduation because I did not want to go to the dance on crutches and I knew Mom could not afford a nice dress for the grad. The day after the grad I found out that I had won two awards: the English Award and the Home Economics Award (for making cute little dresses for my sister).

I may have missed the grad but I still had a good summer. I climbed trees with one leg and left my crutches on the ground propped up against the trunk. I went to the beach with my friend Pam, but found it difficult to use crutches in the sand. I went to movies, concerts and live theatre. I still had hopes of becoming a dancer one day. Also, that summer I met a new boy named Dalton. He took me for a ride on his motorcycle. He visited with me and a few friends in my sun porch. We talked a lot and he was very nice. At the end of summer I was disappointed to discover that he had a girlfriend. Why hadn't he told me? She showed up at my house and threatened to fight me if I didn't stay away from him. Not a problem. I wasn't impressed that he lied to me.

At this time, Ralph was doing weird things that upset Mom. He was selling real estate and had a phone in his car at a time when personal cell phones were science fiction. This was a big deal. He lied and said his company was paying for it for business. One day Bell called Mom and said they were disconnecting our home phone because the bill wasn't paid. She said she would pay it the next day. The lady said, "Do you realize you owe $500?" This was 1967 when the house mortgage was $98 a month.

Then Ralph decided he wanted to build a brick wall across the front of our house next to the sidewalk. There was only about twenty feet from the house to the sidewalk. He started digging a trench one day along the sidewalk edge. It was about three feet deep and two feet wide. A friend came over after dark and fell in the trench with his motorcycle. He wasn't hurt and we weren't sued, but Ralph had to fill in the hole. It was on city property.

Then Ralph decided to put an addition on the back of the house and started digging a hole again. He dug one day and Mom filled it in the next day. He dug it out again. She filled it in again. He next bought a truckload of seed potatoes to start a potato business. She threw them all in the hole he had dug. Yes, it was an interesting summer.

Chapter 8

High School on Crutches

I started high school in 1967 at South Collegiate in London, Ontario, on crutches. I still had the pin in my leg and in 1968 I would have surgery again to have the pin removed. Grade 9 was a decent year. It wasn't like starting any new school before. The difference was that I had friends that were starting with me — there is strength in numbers. Still, they walked in on two legs and I was different.

The insurance claim from the car accident was finally settled, but not very well. Both drivers had the same insurance company, London Life, where Mom worked until the accident, and coincidentally where the other driver worked. We had a lawyer who wasn't very good. Here are the facts as he stated them:

1. The police were busy pulling our family of four out of our car.
2. A nearby garage mechanic pulled the two men out of the other car. The mechanic testified that he could not remember which one was in the driver's seat.
3. One passenger was dead, so could not testify.
4. The other man, Tom Wildgust, refused to testify, but he owned the car. So, Tom's insurance had to pay, but he was not held accountable.

5. Since his insurance company was our insurance company, London Life's goal was to pay as little as possible.
6. If Mom and Ralph did not accept their offer of $98,000 plus $12,000 for me and $1,000 for Alison, then it could be held up in court for years and our medical bills were outstanding.

So they settled. Mom's broken arm never healed well enough for her to go back to her data entry job at London Life, but she heard from a co-worker that Tom Wildgust was bragging about how he got off free of charges. Life just isn't fair.

With some of the money from the settlement our family went on an 18-day Caribbean cruise on the Princess Elizabeth in February of 1968... a silver lining you could say. With the remainder of the money, Ralph bought a run-down restaurant on Horton Street, and Mom and I learned to make diner-style meals and serve customers. Luckily the cook, Elizabeth, a large Hungarian lady, knew what she was doing and helped us a lot. She had lived through Hitler's advancement in WWII and the Nazis had taken over a grand restaurant and estate that her family had owned. She and her daughter had been shipped to a concentration camp. Her stories were chilling and enthralling, and we were grateful for all her help in getting our restaurant going. It was a working man's diner, really. Nothing fancy, but I felt proud that we were the owners.

Mom had my 15th birthday party there. It was just four people I barely knew and a cake. It was a surprise alright, and I guess it was last minute. My best friends couldn't make it and my new boyfriend, Zolton, had to work that afternoon, but he took me to the movies later and gave me a rose. He was sweet and a perfect gentleman. His father was a surgeon.

Around this time, I was working at our restaurant doing dishes in the kitchen, and Ralph was sitting at a table in the corner, talking to a middle-aged gentleman. Something seemed odd about their whispering, but I assumed he was a restaurant supplier. Ralph called me to come over to the table and introduced me to his friend, Mr. Tanner. Pleasantries were exchanged. Then Ralph told me to go with Mr. Tanner. He didn't tell me why, but it didn't matter. I followed Mr. Tanner out to the parking lot, thinking he was going to give me something for the restaurant. He opened the car door and waved me to get in. I thought this was strange but there must be a reason that Ralph told me to go with this man that I knew nothing about. As we drove away I impatiently waited for an explanation. No one spoke for a while. My curiosity was turning into anxiety. I looked down at my shabby skirt and cardigan. I wasn't dressed for meeting anyone or going anywhere. As the car was heading out of town I became very uncomfortable. I kept my head down and clasped my hands tightly in my lap. As we were driving down gravel roads I became scared but was afraid to ask where we were going. My knuckles were growing white. Then Mr. Tanner asked me how I liked school. I said, "Fine." The next few questions were of the nature of small talk to a stranger at a bus stop. Then we were back at the restaurant. The entire drive was about a half hour. He said good-bye and I never saw him again. I can't remember if I told my mom. Why wouldn't I? If I did, I can't remember her response. But I do remember I told Zolton and we talked about it. He thought it was weird. We both thought I was lucky that Mr. Tanner changed his mind about whatever it was he was going to do with me. Maybe he was a talent scout and I failed the test. Maybe he was into child porn and I failed the test. Why was I never told the purpose of the meeting? Why was I afraid to ask?

In the summer of 1968 my left hip was re-opened and the pin removed. As I had suspected all along it made no difference. My left leg was almost two inches shorter than the right leg, and the shortfall was below the knee, not at the hip. The right leg must have grown while the left one was in the cast. The doctors thought that perhaps when I was done growing the left one would catch up. It never did, so I would never be a professional dancer.

But I would still dance for the sheer fun of it. So, I needed to re-configure again. I have always lived by the words of the Serenity Prayer, even before I knew the official quote: to accept the things I cannot change and to change the things I can. (Although I'm not sure that I have the wisdom to know the difference).

I loved where the space program was going and I was keenly interested in computers. I spoke with the guidance counselor in Grade 10 about the possibility of getting into the space program. She did some testing and concluded that my photographic memory and excellent grades could take me anywhere I was determined to go. Whether that was true really doesn't matter. It only matters that I believed her.

From the time we moved to 214 Langley Street in south London in 1964 until we left in 1969, I had some of the best years of my childhood, in spite of the car crash. My closest friends were Holly, Debbie, Darlene, Chris, Roger, Ron, Ted, Zolton, and of course Pam from my old neighbourhood. We rode bikes, climbed trees, played ball, and had plenty of good, clean, outdoor fun. The Tecumseh Public School, South Secondary Collegiate, and a large outdoor public skating rink were across the street from my house. Skating was our favourite winter activity. At that rink in late 1968 I met my first real crush who broke my heart. His name was Don and he was 19 when I was 15. My girlfriend, Holly, had a crush on Don's friend, Howie. Howie was 17 and he worked at the rink. Don had a yellow Ford Mustang with black racing stripes and it was often parked at the rink. I could see it from my house and knew when he was there. Don was always smiling. He was funny and he joked with me like a little sister. I fell hard for him. He made me feel really special.

One night I was walking to the store for milk, when he drove by and offered me a ride. Then he said, "How would you like to go for a drive to the beach?"

I thought, "That's crazy. This is December and it's 7 p.m... so... why not! At least I will get to spend some time with him." So, we drove an hour away to Lake Erie. We sat in the car and watched the waves roll in. He kissed me. I was nervous about what to do if he went further. He didn't. I was disappointed and relieved at the same time. I must give off some kind of body language that makes men nervous. He started the car and drove me home.

I got in the house at 11 p.m. and Mom was hysterical. She sent me out for milk and I returned four hours later. I explained that I went for a drive to Lake Erie with Don.

"You WHAT? We haven't been there since the accident!"

Hmmmm. I hadn't thought of that... "Sorry! Here's the milk."

Don gave me a huge, stuffed lime green elephant for Christmas and asked me to a New Year's Eve party. I really wanted to go, but Mom had other plans. We were going to Stratford. My aunts and uncles were going out on New Year's Eve, and I was babysitting my sister and little cousins. I was really disappointed. When I returned to London in the new year and went to the rink, Don was there with a sexy looking girl of about 19. Her friends were there too and made some cruel comments like, "Come on Don... tell the kid. Don't lead her on." Their relationship became painfully apparent and he attempted to explain. I was embarrassed and ran out of there. Don and Howie followed me in Don's car.

I yelled, "Go away. I hate you!" and threw snowballs at his car (duh). When they drove away I lay down in the snow and cried my heart out.

Holly and I started going back to the rink when Don's car wasn't there. Holly and Howie had never become an item. But after a few weeks Howie was being very comforting to me. He explained a few things about Don and convinced me that it was for the best. Before I knew it Howie was becoming more than just a friend. He would come to my house and we would play Monopoly for hours in my room. Ralph was suspicious and kept checking up on us. But to his surprise we had nothing to hide. Howie's sister, another Diane, was in my class and she tried to tell me Howie had genuine feelings for me. But I knew it would be short-lived because Mom was planning to leave Ralph and move back to Stratford.

The restaurant was going nowhere and Ralph had gone through most of the insurance money. Mom's niece, Carol, and her husband, Bob, (they would play a large role in our future) helped her to find a house in Stratford with rental income from an upstairs apartment. My uncle co-signed for her mortgage since she required this as a single mom. We moved to 204 Front Street in the spring of 1969. Once again, I said good-bye to my London friends. We promised to keep in touch and we did, for a while.

I began at Stratford Central Secondary School in the last month of Grade 10, and one month later had my 16th birthday with my mom, grandma, and two of my aunts. That was sadder than my 15th birthday.

Chapter 9

The 3rd Configuration: A New Start

During my first year back in Stratford I learned a lot. I learned you can't go back. I was not able to re-connect with any of my former friends from Grades 1 to 4. I learned that small towns are a lot more cliquey and dangerous for teenagers. It wasn't easy to make friends in Grade 10. All the kids I met were going steady with one person until they broke up and went steady with another. They were far more liberal with sex, alcohol and drugs, which I had not been exposed to at age 15 in my London group of friends.

I tried to keep in touch with the London group and would occasionally get a ride to London to stay at Holly's house and hang with the old group. There was also Pam, who was still close since our mothers were friends. One day Howie's sister, Diane, called and sadly informed me that her brother Howie had been hit by a car while riding his motorcycle. As he lay dying in the hospital he kept asking for Diane. His mother thought he was asking for his sister, but his sister said she knew he was asking for me. It hurt me deeply that I wasn't there to say good-bye. I wonder how different my life would have been if I had stayed in London. Maybe Howie would still be alive.

Ralph kept coming to our house and interfering. He wanted to connect with Alison but he never came when he said he would. Then he would show up unannounced. He parked his car in a no-parking zone in front of our house and one day another car hit it. Then he was out on the road directing traffic and getting in the way of the police. Mom told him to leave and he wouldn't. He wanted to borrow some money. Mom got upset and he wouldn't go away. I tried to make him leave and he said horrible things to me. I grabbed a butcher knife and threatened him, so he called the police on me. They made him leave. Eventually he stopped coming, but it was poor little Alison who suffered the loss. She missed him and couldn't know what a bad influence he would be. I never wanted him to be alone with her.

Mom got an office job at an automotive parts factory. I got a part-time job in the kitchen at the hospital, and I acquired my driver's license. Alison was five and starting kindergarten and I was in Grade 11.

I began to make friends at school. Susan, Sandy and Luanne were crazy friends and we had hilarious times together. Every day after school we met at a cafe for Coke and a cigarette. Yes, I started to smoke and I learned to inhale. We went roller-skating at the arena every chance we got. That was a great place to meet boys and hang out. Grandma had moved to a new apartment and purchased a six-pack of beer for the movers. There were two bottles left in her fridge for almost a year. At the end of Grade 11 I sweetly conned her into giving me the two beers for a graduation celebration, just two bottles for four girls to have a toast. I put them in my roller skates to take to the arena on a Friday night.

I didn't realize that Mom was suspicious. She saw the beer in my skates but said nothing. I met my friends at the arena and the four of us shared the two beers before skating. We sat in the car with a sock around the bottle so that no one would know what we were drinking (another duh — who drinks out of a sock?).

Well, about an hour later a friend skated by me and said, "Hey... your Mom's here and wants to talk to you." I saw her at the on-ramp of the rink, tapping her foot and pressing her lips together. I skated up to her. She grabbed me by the arm and pulled me outside, nearly knocking me off my feet. Of course, we had a crowd watching.

"What did you do with the beer?"

"What beer?" (Wrong answer).

"I saw the beer in your skate and followed you here. Where is it?"

"A few friends were having a toast for a special celebration. It's gone."

"Where did you get it?"

"From Grandma."

"MY MOTHER!" she screamed. "Get in the car. We're going home."

I was never so scared of her, but had also never had reason to be. She was furious with me. She said that she had first called Bob (my cousin who worked as a police dispatcher) and asked him to have the police arrest me to scare the hell out of me. But he said, "No Pat, she will have a record."

I could have been in jail! Actually, I was almost 17 at that time and beer wasn't the worst thing. I had been going to parties where we drank rye and Coke, and occasionally smoked weed. I got sick from the rye and the joint made me dizzy and want to eat Oh Henry! chocolate bars until there were none left at the store.

The summer before Grade 12 was a wild one. I had spending money from working at the hospital and a car to drive (occasionally). I drove to Holly's cottage in Bayfield for a few days and, while I was there, dated a wealthy jeweler's son twice, but I didn't like the hickeys he gave. That was the summer of 1970 when Pam and I were very foolish. We almost had an accident driving on the curves of Snake Road in Ipperwash. Laughing and speeding we passed a cube van on the wrong side of the road. But that summer there were other incidents too.

Pam's mom had a small old British car for bombing around the beach. It had been painted blue and decorated with huge, brightly coloured flower stickers. It was as cute as a button. She let me drive it since Pam was not yet 16. We kept jumper cables in the trunk, as we often had to get a boost to start it. On the road between Ipperwash and Grand Bend we never had a shortage of lads willing to stop and lend a hand. Grand Bend was a hot place to party at the beach and roller skate at night.

On one occasion Pam had a terrible toothache. I drove her 20 minutes away to Forest to see her dentist. He did some work and gave her two pain pills just in case. We decided to share them. Bad idea! Since I didn't have pain, I got dizzy on the drive back. Pam had pain so she didn't get dizzy, so I let her drive, even though she didn't have a license (she was only 14). She got us back safe and sound.

On another occasion, I had permission to drive Mom's car to visit Pam at the beach. Pam had a boyfriend named Mike, a Native living on the Ipperwash reserve. We often hung out with his friends. This particular day — I don't remember where we were all going — but the boys drove in a big old Lincoln, and we were following them in my mom's Ford Fairlane. Driving down bumpy dirt roads, the boys kept going faster and I kept up with them, the girls cheering me on. The next bump sent us airborne and we landed with no brakes! I pumped the brake pedal to no avail and could only steer, hoping for no need to stop, as we gradually slowed down on the approach to the next little town. We had lost the boys' car and were panicking while searching for a mechanic, all the while turning corners rather than going through a stop sign. We saw a garage but had to circle the block twice before slowing to a stop on the property. It was about closing time on a Saturday evening. The mechanic quickly determined that the brake had been knocked off the wheel. He quoted what it would cost to fix. We had very little money between all four of us. We were stranded, scared and desperate. The quote was not that high, but we just didn't have enough money. I explained our situation and he offered to fix it if we babysat for him that evening. We agreed wholeheartedly. In half an hour the car was fine again and it was time to pay up...

"Please, please, please let us go," we pleaded as sweetly and seductively as four teenage girls can be. What a great guy! He smiled and said, "Away you go." We were so grateful and so fortunate that the car was fixed and we weren't hurt. We drove slowly back home and counted our blessings. God was watching over us.

The summer was not over yet. Back in Stratford four of us girls decided to camp at Wildwood for one night. We pitched a tent in the afternoon and then went into town for dinner and to the roller rink. When we left the rink at 11 p.m., black thunderclouds were rolling across the sky. We arrived at the campsite to find our tent flattened by the strong winds, and everything inside was drenched in the pouring rain. We scrambled to recover what we could. Our friend Maddy lost a tooth cap in the dark commotion inside the collapsed tent. Then she tried to help the handsome, young, naked man in the next campsite who was struggling to stabilize his tent in the drenching rain. His wife was yelling for him to come back inside. It was funny to watch. We sat in the car stuffed with wet blankets and camping gear and talked and drank until the sun came up. It was a real bonding experience.

I wasn't always able to borrow Mom's car because she needed it for work. Summers could be long and hot. Near Wildwood Park there was a deep quarry in the village of St. Marys. It was a popular swimming hole going back to 1935 when the limestone quarry filled up with water. It is Canada's largest outdoor swimming pool. Having no wheels, Susan and I decided to try to hitchhike the 12 miles to the quarry. While walking along highway #7 with thumbs out, a pickup truck stopped with three scruffy workers in the front seat.

"Where you going ladies?"

"To the Quarry to meet some friends," we replied.

"Hop in."

"Hop in where?" we asked.

"We can make room. Do you want a ride or not?"

Foolishly, we climbed in and sat on the knees of the two passengers beside the driver. I remember thinking we probably shouldn't be doing this. We chatted about our boyfriends who were waiting for us. There were no cell phones in those days for emergency calls and we actually had no boyfriends waiting for us. We did make it to the quarry unscathed and with our virtues intact. Luckily, we met up with friends who gave us a ride back home later. That would not be the last time I would get into a truck with strangers.

In Grade 12, I met Kay, my new best local friend. I changed my persona with Kay. She was more mature and not into drugs. We got along great and we went to parties but drank more sensibly.

In those days at Central Secondary School the dress code did not allow girls to wear jeans or dress pants of any kind — only skirts and dresses. One cold winter day I wore a pair of corduroy pants with a blouse and vest. I managed to get through the entire day until the last class, which was math with Mr. Robins. Upon entering the classroom he asked me if the dress code had changed or if I had permission to wear pants. Since I did not, he sent me to the office. I sat down and had a mature chat with the vice principle, Mr. Sinclair. We discussed the pros and cons of wearing pants versus dresses, the climate, respect for culture, and "if boys could wear pants then why not girls?" The next morning the school announcements included a dress code change allowing girls to wear dress pants (but not jeans). I felt like a hero... a pioneer... a somebody!

Early in 1970 I applied to the courts to advance me some money from my accident trust fund to pay for flying lessons. The Stratford Airport allowed lessons from the age of 16. Imagine that: when my friends were learning to drive I was learning to fly. Bruce Dale was an excellent instructor. If I remember correctly I started ground school and shortly after began flying a Cessna 150 single engine. I loved it. There was a lot to learn about clouds, weather, physics, velocity, thrust and equipment. It did not take long to pass my written exam. Now I just had to put in the required hours of experience and do the flight tests. I still wanted to be an astronaut and I took my flight lessons seriously.

PART II

Chapter 10

The 4th Configuration: Marriage

At the age of 17 I met a man three years older and fell in love. Seven months later I was pregnant. The day after I turned 18, the legal age of majority was lowered from 21 to 18. Now I was of age to drink, vote, access what was left of my trust fund, and I was about to be a wife and a mom and I hadn't even attended my Grade 12 graduation yet. I quit flying lessons and applied the unused refund to furniture. We were happy and looking forward to starting our family.

My husband was 21 to my 18 years. We both had a lot of growing up to do. In hindsight, I realize that I still had a child mentality and left my mother's home for my father-like husband's home. I was obedient rather than an equal, but it was not his fault. It was in my character not to be confrontational. We had love and emotional support from both our families. We still liked to party and I struggled to keep up. In the 1970s there were no warnings about pregnancy and alcohol or tobacco. I drank less alcohol and smoked less tobacco because it made me feel sick. I was growing away from my friends who were either single and going to school, or married and moving away.

Our baby was due at the end of January. Mom lived about a kilometre across town and on a sunny winter's day I decided a healthy walk to Mom's would be nice. The quickest way to cross town was near the railway station. It was slow walking in deep snow with heavy boots, wearing a heavy sheepskin coat, and carrying an eight-month fetus. I was tired by the time I approached the tracks and I was only halfway there. In front of me were about four or five train tracks to cross and the middle one had a freight train that stretched as far as I could see both ways. I thought about whether I should head east or west for the shortest route around this train that did not appear to be moving anytime soon. There was no one around. I have been around enough trains to know they chug and puff and clang before they ever start to move. My mind was racing. There was a three-foot clearance under the train. I hesitated about two minutes and weighed all my options. Then I crouched over and crawled under that big old freight train, my heart racing. I made it! Not another train in sight. I had renewed energy to walk the rest of the way to Mom's. I was not going to tell her what I did, BUT when I arrived she saw a big black grease mark on the back of my white sheepskin coat. I had to explain it. She was angry.

Preparing for motherhood, I relied entirely on the advice of my mother, my grandma, my mother-in-law and my Aunt Marie. This was the norm. I went to prenatal classes and guess who my classmate was? It was my former health and Phys-Ed teacher! She taught us about sex and protection. She must have thought I wasn't paying attention in class. I was embarrassed but she was so very gracious and non-judgemental. To make it more uncomfortable, her husband was Mom's boss at work. I knew him from the company Christmas parties and summer picnics. These types of encounters made me feel naked and ashamed about being pregnant.

In late January I was just past my due date and could not put my boots on anymore. I had gained 40 pounds and was only 5 feet, 2 inches tall. Mom talked me into taking castor oil to bring on the labour. She mixed it with orange juice and told me to drink it. So, I tasted her big glass of orange castor oil potion, and I gagged.

"Just drink it down all at once, don't taste it!" she insisted. I drank about half of it and threw up in the toilet. What does she say?

"Damn it all anyway that's not gonna do you any good. Here finish it!"

And I did. Then we went for a drive on a bumpy gravel road on January 30. That night I went into labour and my beautiful baby girl was born on January 31, 1972.

Chapter 11

New Baby: Instructions Not Included!

Tina Patricia weighed 7 pounds, 8 ounces and she was perfect. We were in the hospital for five days. The babies stayed in the nursery and the moms went there to feed them or hold them. There were seven or eight babies in the nursery but only one mother was breast-feeding. She was a Mennonite lady. In those days the popular feeding method was glass bottles or Playtex Nurser bottles and formula. Very few women nursed or expressed milk for bottles. In hindsight I wish I would have tried nursing. Mom tried to nurse me but her milk was too weak. She had an awful time, so she cautioned me against breast-feeding.

When we brought Tina home we took great care to make everything comfortable for her. In the daytime we put her bassinet near the stereo so she would like music and not be bothered by soft noises when sleeping. Her doctor suggested, at seven days old, that I start giving her one teaspoon of rice pablum mixed with her evening bottle in order to encourage her to start sleeping through the night. This worked well, but you know what they say about the best laid plans. On about my fifth evening at home we went to bed with one glass bottle of formula made up in the fridge. During the night Tina awoke and I warmed up her bottle in a pot of water on the stove (no microwave ovens yet). Feeling totally confident in my new role, I took Tina to the living room to change her and give her eager little mouth the bottle. Then I carried her to the bathroom as I felt a surge of blood run down my leg. The maternity pad I was wearing was saturated. As I tried to sit on the toilet while holding her, the glass bottle rolled from baby's mouth and smashed on the floor. Tina was startled and began screaming. On the floor was blood and formula mixed with broken glass and I was in my bare feet. What do I do first? My poor baby was hungry and there was no more formula made up. It was probably 15 or 20 minutes before there was another bottle of formula made to feed my hungry, screaming baby. That was definitely the worst night we had. Tina was a good baby and taught me a lot about being a mother.

We lived in the apartment for less than a year before we were able to buy a 1½-storey house with two bedrooms on Caledonia Street in Stratford. Next, we got a St. Bernard puppy named Stratford's Lady Prudence (we called her Poo). Tina learned to walk while hanging onto Poo's fur coat. But before she could walk, Tina had a round baby walker with a seat and four tiny wheels that she could motor around in by pushing her feet on the floor. Like many children in those walkers she rolled down the basement stairs in it, staying upright and unharmed all the way to the bottom. Needless to say, those walkers are now banned in Canada for safety reasons.

A terrifying incident around that time was when I locked myself out of the house with Tina and Poo inside. Tina was in her walker and the basement door was securely closed. I took a basket of laundry out the back door to hang on the line and the door locked behind me. Through the window I could see Tina in her walker. My mind raced as to what to do to open the door. I ran next door and called Mom. She called the police and then drove to my house. When the policeman arrived he was very young and nonchalant, totally unaware of the imminent danger. He tried the door and said, "It's locked."

"Yes," I said. "I need you to open it, my daughter is in there!"

He looked through the window and said, "There's a kid in there".

"Yes, break it open please," I said.

"Why don't you get her to open it?" he said.

"WHAT! She's a baby in a walker. She can't even reach the latch. Can't you find a way to get in?"

He looked through the window again and said with a worried tone, "There's a dog in there."

I assured him the dog would not hurt him. He asked if there was another way in. There is a door from the garage into the back porch. It had only a hook latch that could be busted with enough pressure. The cop hesitantly went into the garage and busted the latch off the old wooden door. I was so relieved my child was still safe. Poo took good care of Tina. It's scary how quickly the unexpected can happen.

In the spring of 1973, when Tina was one year old, I discovered I was pregnant again. *We* were not pregnant, *I* was pregnant and neither of us was prepared to have another baby. I was not in a good place emotionally. We were trying to fix up our house with various cosmetic projects. I was picking up small jobs — at the post office for the Christmas rush, as a school crossing guard (taking Tina with me in her stroller), selling Coppercraft decor at evening home parties when Mom could babysit, and I even worked for a few weekends as a server at the Avon Hotel on Saturday nights when they had strippers dancing. The tips were good but the ambience was not. Around closing time a fight would break out. I quit that job after about six shifts.

We were just trying to make ends meet. I was quite upset and worried about being pregnant again and what this would do to our relationship. My doctor arranged for a legal abortion at a hospital in London, Ontario. On the weekend before the medical procedure I miscarried the baby. In my opinion it was an act of God. I started to bleed. Mom came to stay with Tina. My cousin Carol and her husband came to my rescue again. Bob is eight years my senior and he escorted me to the hospital. At the triage desk we told the nurse what was happening. She asked if Bob was "the father." In sync we said "No" and I added, "He's my cousin" at the same time as he said "I'm her uncle." Well that was awkward! The nurse just nodded and said, "Not important." I was admitted and it was all over in 48 hours.

By the fall of that year I found myself pregnant again. This time was different. I was ready for it and happy about it. In my heart I felt that my husband resented my being pregnant.

Often, I felt like he was punishing me. He wanted to paint the exterior siding of the house and insisted on my helping with it in the spring of 1974 when I was in my third trimester. The smell of the paint made me nauseous. We argued about it. We still had a parent-child relationship. I didn't feel that I had the right to simply refuse so I whined about it. To this day I still have to mentally fight to give myself the right to say "NO." Unfortunately this problem surfaced many times through my life. If I could give my children and grandchildren only one word of advice, it would be to respect and love themselves. I still struggle with that.

Our second child was due in early July, but I had gained 50 pounds, and the curve in my spine from the previous broken hip was giving me grief. The doctor suggested we try to bring on labour two weeks early. I went into hospital all day Friday with false labour and no dilation. The plan was to go home and try again a week later. My husband had planned a fishing trip with his father and brother to my uncle's fish camp up north.

"Do you want me to cancel the trip and stay with you?" he said.

Of course I did! However I said, "No, you can go. The labour may not start again, and then you would have missed the trip." I wanted him to say, "I want to stay with you just in case the baby is born." But he didn't.

Friday came and he pulled our van up in front of the hospital. He said good-bye to me without even getting out of the driver's seat. I opened my own door and heaved myself out, suitcase in hand, and waddled up the sidewalk as he drove off. I felt terribly alone. In the hospital I was in labour most of that day and Adam was born around 6 p.m. He weighed 8 pounds, 6 ounces. The nurse swaddled my baby and laid him in my arms, just the two of us bonding. It was an incredible experience. The song "You and Me Against the World" came into my head.

Adam John was born on June 28, 1974. Two days later was my 21st birthday. Interestingly, I was again in the hospital on another milestone birthday, but this time with my son.

By the time Adam was one year old, we sold the house in Stratford and bought a three-bedroom brick bungalow in Sebringville. We had great neighbours and we joined the community centre. Both Tina and Adam started school while living there. In fact, we would maybe still be there had we not gotten divorced.

Chapter 12

Granny and the Beer Truck

Uncle Red and Aunt Eunice were my cousin Judy's parents. I spent a good deal of time with Judy in my adolescent summers. She was six years older than me and theoretically was taking care of me from time-to-time. That didn't stop us from getting into awkward situations like destroying Mom's cookware trying to make homemade candy, or causing Granny Roth to miss her flight to Seattle after putting her on a beer truck to the airport. Yes, this I have to explain.

I think it was the summer of 1976. Granny was 80 years old and because she had great-grandchildren we renamed her Granny Roth to distinguish her from the new grandmas. She was invited to fly to Seattle to visit her eldest daughter, and Judy and I were tasked with the responsibility of getting her to the airport on time. Uncle Red owned a garage and had a fancy, solid automobile tuned up to make sure we had no problems for the two-hour drive on the 401 highway to Toronto. Aunt Eunice was taking care of our babies so that we had no distractions — just Granny and her luggage.

Half-way to Toronto Judy's car began to slow down. The gas gauge was on empty. When the mechanic said the car was ready to go, she assumed the tank was full too. It was not. We pulled over to the shoulder of the 401 highway in the middle of nowhere. In a panic we tried to think of what to do. We didn't want to upset Granny. She gets red in the face when her blood pressure goes up. Keep calm Granny. We'll stop a car and get some help.

We really could have used the cell phone invention that day. Young people today have no idea how to stay calm and be resilient in an emergency. It's not easy to stop a car on the 401 that's going 110 km/h. After about 15 minutes a little old pickup truck with a little old driver stopped.

"I am going as far as the next town. I can take someone there to get gas, but I can't bring them back," he said.

"Go with him Diane!" Judy insisted.

Nervously, I hopped in his truck and away we went. About 20 minutes down the road he took a turn off the highway and there was a garage, but nothing else. He dropped me off and told the attendant why I was there.

"I can sell you a container of gas, but I can't leave the garage," the attendant said. "There's no one else here."

After a few minutes another guy came into the store to buy something and the attendant asked him if he had time to drive me back where I came from. He looked annoyed but agreed. I felt as if I was being passed around without my consent, but I was grateful for the help. So off I went in this last guy's car.

Meanwhile back on the highway, a huge fourteen-wheeler Molson Beer truck had stopped to help out. Apparently, the driver and Judy boosted Granny up into the truck and he headed off to the airport with her before I got back. We gassed up the car and resumed our trip towards the airport. Then Judy realized that we still had Granny's luggage in our trunk!

Judy was speeding, trying to catch up to Granny's truck.

"There it is!" she said.

As she pulled up beside it, I was flailing my arms to tell him to pull over. The truck started gearing down and Judy got a better look. It wasn't the right truck.

Away we sped leaving him in her dust. This happened two more times. Then as we were approaching the off ramp towards the airport, a police car with lights flashing was tailing us. I can't remember if the siren was on, probably not. Judy would not stop because we had to find Granny, and her flight would be boarding now.

We drove around in the parking garage looking for a spot to park, followed by the police with flashing lights. As Judy pulled into a spot the cruiser stopped behind her. We all got out of the cars. Heading for the luggage in the trunk, Judy told the officer, "Give me a ticket if you want. I don't have time to stop. My grandma is going to miss her plane." The cop looked at me. I was 22 years old, wearing short pink hot pants, and my long blonde hair was tied with ribbons in two pigtails.

"This is your grandma?" he sarcastically asked.

Judy scoffed. "No. Of course not. My grandma came in a beer truck!"

The cop was stunned. We took off with the luggage and headed for the departures. The cop just followed us. We found Granny, but the plane had left. The cop gave Judy a ticket. We managed to book Granny on another plane five hours later. We found a phone booth and called Aunt Eunice in Stratford to call Aunt Edith in Seattle and tell her what time to meet Granny's next plane. Then we stayed to see her onto the plane. We were never again chosen to escort her to anything important.

However, when I got my first car, a cheap used Austin American, Granny Roth and my kids were often with me when it wouldn't start. I always carried jumper cables and Granny got used to the process of getting her going so that we could get home before dark. She stayed calm and encouraged me, saying that I was a smart girl and all would be fine.

Chapter 13

My Regrets

In hindsight, I think we were too strict with our children but they were rarely spanked. A spanking was a tap on the bottom that got their attention and hurt their ego. They knew by the tone of our voices when we were serious. But some instances stand out in my memory and tear at my heartstrings with regret.

We had a policy of not allowing our children to climb into bed with us. We did not want to start a habit that was hard to break. At age two, Adam went through a stage at bedtime of crying and wanting Mommy to lie with him. I read him a book and then left the room. He cried himself to sleep and that really bothered me. I sat on the floor outside his door watching the clock. It was current theory that I should let him cry for up to 20 minutes before going back in the room. He generally was asleep by then. He got over it in a couple of months, but it was the hardest thing to hear my baby cry for me. I believed that I was bearing the pain in order to do the best thing for him. If I gave in to him, it would be even harder to break the cycle the next time.

When I think of what I would do differently in life if I could change history, there are two specific events that come to mind — one concerns Tina and one concerns Adam. When Tina was four she became very sick in the middle of the night and I had no idea just how sick she was. I had been sleeping and something woke me up. I thought I heard whimpering in Tina's room.

A few minutes later, Tina entered our bedroom and said, "Mommy my head hurts."

"Go back to bed," her father said.

"But I'm thirsty," she said.

I made an attempt to get up but he said, "NO. She just needs to go to sleep. Tina, if you're thirsty get a drink of water."

Tina left the room without another word so I thought she was going back to bed. The next morning I found her lying on the hall floor with an unopened bottle of ginger ale. She had a high fever and was lethargic. I was so angry with myself that I had not tended to her when she needed me. I cuddled her in my arms and laid her in my bed while waiting for the doctor. He diagnosed Tina with scarlet fever. Damn it! Why didn't I follow my instincts? Why was my immediate reaction to do as I was told? Maybe because I hated confrontation. Maybe because I just didn't know how to be a good mother. I never forgave myself for that and I remained silently angry with him.

The second incident that I cannot forget was many years later when I was a single mom. Adam was eight years old. I had a small apartment with my two kids. Adam and Tina each had a bedroom, and I slept in the living room. I was struggling financially and emotionally. Adam had a mess of stuff all over his room and I asked him to tidy it up before he went out to play. In two minutes he said it was done. I went in to check and saw that the junk was all gone. I opened his closet door and a pile tumbled to the floor, including a partially cut-up cereal box. I was livid and screamed at him, "Get rid of all this garbage!" and I threw the cereal box at the bedroom door. His expression grew from scared to sad.

He picked up the cereal box and whispered, "You weren't supposed to see this. It's your Mother's Day present. I made you a recipe box."

My breath left my lungs. I fell to my knees and I could see that the box had been carefully cut out so that the front was shorter than the back and it was the perfect size to store recipes. How could I have jumped to conclusions and been so mean? He was so sweet when he asked me if I liked it. I loved it more than you could know.

It seems my most prominent memories are of the bad stuff, the stuff you have to live with, the stuff you regret the most, the stuff that has the biggest impact on who you see when you look in the mirror, the stuff you have to forgive yourself for in order to move forward.

Chapter 14

The Beginning of the End

An opportunity knocked on my door in 1977. My cousin Carol, who managed a Kwikie Minit Market, asked me if I would like to manage another store that was opening in Stratford. The compensation was a percentage of the profits. I would need transportation because we still lived five miles away in Sebringville. This opportunity would change my life in ways I could never have imagined.

I had no previous business experience but Carol taught me everything I needed to know about running a convenience store. Most of the customers were local and I got to know them by name. I purchased a used car and my Aunt Marie babysat my kids as well as Carol's kids while we were at our stores. I enjoyed the bookkeeping and sales aspects but managing people did not come easy for me. I had one full-time adult, and a few part-time teenagers for the evening shifts. As I mentioned before, I shun away from confrontation, so discipline and even constructive criticism made me anxious, and they were usually followed by my apology of sorts.

I didn't make a lot of money at the store, but the freedom and independence gave me a new feeling of accomplishment and confidence. I interacted with people of all ages and walks of life, and finally really felt like an adult. A cute little boy named JD came into my store regularly with his big sisters to buy candy. Little did I know that one day, as a teenager, he would meet, fall in love with, and eventually marry my daughter.

Having a car and a job made it possible for me to enroll Tina and Adam in dance lessons and sports. I also enrolled in adult ballet and jazz just for fun. By January of 1978 we were financially in a position to take our first trip ever outside of Ontario.

We flew to Hawaii for two weeks and Mom kept the children. Hawaii was amazing, but we argued a lot. The first day I forgot to bring the camera on a sightseeing trip. The second day I brought the camera but forgot to put film in it... and so it went. Everything that went wrong was my fault. One day we went our separate ways. I went to the beach by myself and was very sad that we were not getting along. Then I heard a van approaching, with a loud speaker that was announcing "Everyone out of the water! The Portuguese Man of War is attacking!" This made me extremely excited. I was looking out in the water for ships. I didn't know until later that the Portuguese Man of War were jellyfish with stingers. I think I was associating it with the attack at Pearl Harbor. Nevertheless, I loved Hawaii.

I managed the store for less than two years. Having to drive back and forth from Sebringville whenever there was a problem at the store was a hassle. Sometimes the store safe would not open or would not close. Sometimes the alarm would go off after hours and I would have to do a walk around with the police to check the premises. Sometimes a student didn't show up for a shift. Then there was Austin. He was a local that came into my store and we chatted. He was very nice and very charismatic and changed the course of my life.

One evening at home the phone rang. To my surprise, it was Austin. He was at the Sebringville Hotel and invited my husband and me to join him for a drink. I wanted them to meet.

"You go ahead," he said. "You know him, I don't."

I was shocked. I felt uneasy about going without him, but when he insisted, I decided I wanted to go because it was exciting. We never went out to the hotel on a weeknight. Going out on my own to meet a friend for a drink was something I hadn't done since I was married, not even with a girlfriend.

I went and enjoyed an hour of idle conversation. It was exhilarating and Austin was charming. I was attracted to him but told myself I would not cross over the line. He was a perfect gentleman and after that I ran into him spontaneously downtown where he offered to show me through a building he was renovating. I took my kids to the park and saw him going to a concert. He played drums and invited me to see his photos taken with Randy Bachman of the band BTO. He knew my love for music and invited me several times to see musicians at a local hotel. He seemed to know them personally. Never once did he make any moves on me or try to kiss me, but he was filling a void in my life.

It's not that I didn't love my husband. I never felt like a woman with him. In addition, there had been several women in his life that I felt unable to compete with. They were not women that I thought he would leave me for, but they were women that he enjoyed being around. I felt taken for granted. I wanted to feel the way I did when I was around Austin.

I thought about leaving. There's a lot to consider when you have two small children who are six and four. He was a good father and a good provider - just a bad fit for me. He wasn't physically abusive and the children loved their father. The problem was with me. I was growing increasingly unsatisfied with a life that had been fine for six years. I was maturing.

In 1978, I gave up managing the Kwikie store in Stratford and got a clerical job at the factory where Mom worked. We tried marriage counselling for a while, to no avail. In 1980 I left, rented an apartment in Stratford and took the children with me. After a couple of months, I was laid off my job. Immediately I took a job as a waitress. He convinced me things would be better if I just moved back home and tried again. We reconciled and immediately arranged for beautiful family photos.

Life was better for a while. I met a girl named Jikki and she became a close friend. Jikki was in her early twenties, had never been married, and owned a hairstyling business. I admired her. She was her own woman. She helped me to gain confidence and take risks. We went skydiving together at the Grand Bend Airport. It was both terrifying and exhilarating. We were both on a natural high - until we got home.

As time went by our relationship slowly deteriorated. I have been reminded that this part of our history was laid to rest many years ago. There are two sides to every story and reality is somewhere between. To protect the privacy of some who have different versions of events, I have chosen to leave the remainder of this chapter unpublished.

Chapter 15

The 5th Configuration: Single with Two Kids

Two years after reconciling I moved out again with my kids, this time for good. We moved to an apartment in Stratford and shortly after I was laid off my job once again.

In need of income to pay rent and put food on the table, I took a four week dog-grooming course and began my own grooming business, sneaking dogs in and out of my apartment. In 1984 I petitioned for divorce on grounds of irreconcilable differences. It was granted in 1985. Pam and I reconnected. I began going out to clubs and bars with Jikki, Mom, co-workers, and I was meeting several new men. Some were nice and some not so nice. Unfortunately, I was still a follower and could not bring myself to say NO if the situation got uncomfortable. I just clenched my fists and pretended it wasn't happening. It would be a few years yet before I gained enough respect for myself to break that mold. I hated those men, and I hated myself.

I have agonized over including this chapter in my memoirs. I have never talked about this with anyone. I feel I have to be brutally honest if I am ever to rid myself of this guilt. So, I will bury it here and hope my loved ones will forgive me. There were four times when a man was on top of me and I hated it, I hated him, and I hated myself because I had no voice. Once it was in a tent and I was scared because my children were asleep nearby. My girlfriend and I had just met these two lads near our campsite and they offered us a beer. One thing led to another, then it happened. I could not stop it. I could only think, "Oh God please don't let my children wake up." It was not rape. I did not try to stop it. I wanted it to stop but I could not find a voice or move a muscle. I have since learned that you have to love yourself to respect yourself.

Chapter 16

Everything Happens for a Reason

They say everyone comes into your life for a reason, a season, or a lifetime. Austin came into my life for a reason. Al came into my life for a season. I was at a bar in Tavistock with my Mom and her friend Jane. Jane's husband was playing in the band that night. Al asked me to dance and we immediately had chemistry. He asked if he could call me the next weekend for a date. He was so pleasant that I gave him my phone number.

When I told Mom his name and where he lived, she figured out that he was my third cousin. His mother and mine were first cousins. I had never met that branch of my family on Grandpa Roth's side. The next weekend Al came with his sister and her date to pick me up.

"Guess what?" I said. "We're related."

He was shocked. So was his sister, Sonia. Apparently, that had happened to him before.

Al and I got along famously. We dated and had great fun. I got to know all his clan and friends in Tavistock. His sister, Janice, and I became good friends during my single life stage. My children loved to play with her children and we spent a great deal of time at the farm where she lived with Tom. In fact, I became close with all of Janice's family who were actually distant cousins. My feelings for Al grew intensely. He was a good man, respectful and honourable. He was also single and had been hurt before by a woman. He was cautious. Although we never talked about our future, I knew that he deserved a full family life with children, and I could never give him that. Or maybe he just liked me and didn't love me. I was getting mixed signals from him.

I turned 30 in 1983, and was single and living with my two children in a small apartment. Fortunately, I was rehired at American Motors in finance where I had previously worked with Mom. My divorce was being finalized and I would be coming into my share of the settlement. My sister, Alison, was going to be heading off to college so Mom and I decided to buy a house together and share expenses. We bought a three-bedroom semi-detached home on Devon Street. Mom and Alison shared a bedroom, Tina and I shared a bedroom, and Adam had his own room. Al and his friends helped us move. Life was fairly stable for a few years. Mom finally met a very nice gentleman named Paul and they dated for three years before he died from a sudden heart attack.

At school Tina was evaluated as being artistically gifted. I had known of her talents before she ever started school. Tina later went on to win a scholarship to the Ontario College of Art and Design (OCAD) in Toronto. After graduating she worked as a graphic designer, developing identities and packaging for leading companies including Tim Hortons. Coincidentally, Adam was evaluated as being intellectually gifted. He performed very well as a public speaker and debater in high school and he was a contestant throughout secondary school on the television show *Reach for the Top*. It was a trivia question competition between secondary schools, and Adam's area of expertise was geography and science. He went on to Concordia University in Montreal and studied journalism. He speaks several languages and teaches English in Japan. I have always been extremely proud of both my children.

As for me, I was working, playing slow-pitch ball and living life. However, I was having neck and back pain from a curved spine which resulted from my old broken hip and short leg. The chiropractor suggested I see a surgeon in London, Ontario who was experimenting with leg lengthening of bones. I was approved for surgery and my boss approved a leave of absence from my job. The procedure was to make a seven-inch incision in my outer left thigh and slice through the middle of the femur bone. An 18-inch sliding bar made of one-inch thick steel would be screwed into the femur bone along the outside of my leg. After surgery, I would remain in the hospital for two to four weeks. Each day the doctor would turn a tap on the end of the steel bar and the bar would lengthen a tiny bit. This in turn would spread apart the bone a millimetre or so. The goal was to spread the bone a total of 1.5 inches over several weeks. The daily procedure had to be minimal because all the tissue, veins, muscles, etc. had to be lengthened, as well as the bone. The tap on the end of the bar was attached to steel-toothed cogs that were attached to steel pins that were screwed into either side of the cut bone. You have no idea how strong and tight a muscle that attaches to the femur bone is. The daily procedure did not hurt, but it felt very tense.

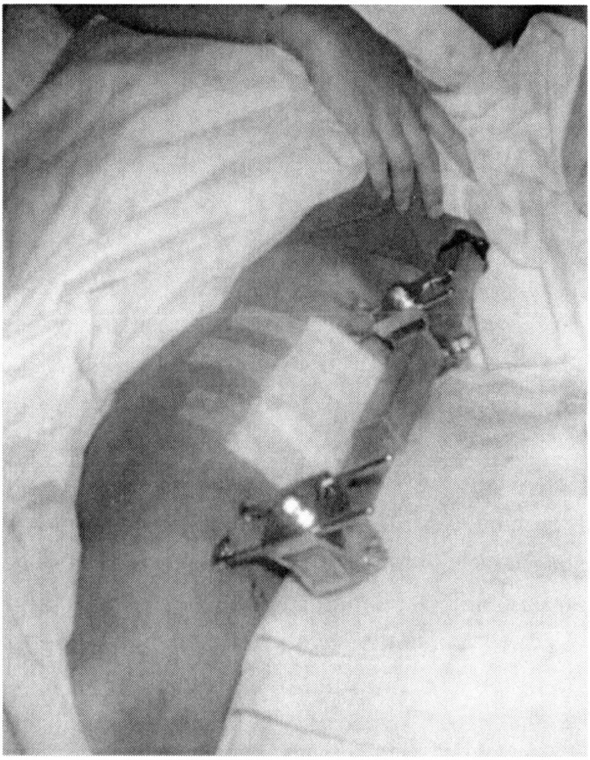

After surgery, with steel bar attached to femur bone by four steel pins

I could get out of bed to use the bathroom as long as I didn't bear any weight on my left leg with the bar attached. About ten days into the process I was attempting to slide back onto the bed and I heard the sound of steel grinding on steel. I knew it was my leg and called the nurse. She took one look and ran out calling for assistance. A male nurse and an aid came and called for a doctor. The teeth of the steel cogs were slipping and grinding on each other due to the pull of the muscle. I felt extreme pain and numbness at the same time. I was assisted into the bed while trying not to move the bar any more than it had already. I was given a shot of Demerol and a wet towel to clench between my teeth while the doctor tried to loosen the steel bar from the pins and get the cogs back into place. The male nurse fainted and was removed. I was taken down to surgery and the process was started over because the gain in millimetres was lost.

Over the several weeks I was in hospital I had surgery three times and became addicted to morphine. I will never forget that moment when I needed something for pain and the doctor put his nose close to mine, stared into my eyes and said, "If I give you any more medication you will turn blue and die!" I was cut off the morphine. That was literally the worst night of my life. I thought I was dying. In the morning the sun shone in the window, I heard birds singing, and I was alive. The horror was gone. Since then I am very cautious in taking pain medication for anything. I would rather die than have an addiction like that again.

Before I left the hospital another surgery was performed to remove the bar and pins, and attach a steel plate to hold the separated bone in place while it was mending. Bone chips were carved from my upper hip to fill in the one-inch space in my femur that was created by the lengthening procedure. I would need to use crutches for at least six months and put no weight on my left leg until the bone was mended and strong. By this time, I had become very capable of getting around on crutches and returned to work. Thankfully my two pre-teen children were understanding and cooperative. They were doing well at school, helping me at home, and I had help from Mom who still lived with me. On the day I came home from hospital, Alison, Tina, and Adam made a Jello dessert to surprise me. They had seen Jello salads made with mini-marshmallows, so they decided it would be special to make red Jello with gummy bears. When they went to the fridge to present their dish, to our surprise there was no Jello in the bowl. It was a bowl full of extraordinarily enlarged gummy bears that looked like Pillsbury Dough Boys. The bears had soaked up all the Jello. We all laughed hysterically at it.

PART III

Chapter 17

My Soul Mate

It was the summer of 1984 and with crutches under my arms I joined my girlfriends and went to Al's slow pitch ball tournaments. His team was called "The Tavistock Two-Fours." Through Al, I was friends with all the players and their girlfriends. Now I will tell you the reason I believe Al came into my life.

There was a new outfielder playing for Tavistock. He was an incredible athlete in my opinion. He could run faster, slide farther, and catch any ball in the outfield. He happened to be the brother of my girlfriend Sherri. I had known Sherri for a few years. Her boyfriend played on Al's ball team and Sherri had worked with my friend Jikki. I learned that Sherri's brother was John Lyoness. Years later I learned that we had met once before, in kindergarten at Juliet school, when he came to school one day in his brother's place.

We were having a beer after the ball game at the end of August, 1984. Several of the couples were planning a canoe trip on the Labour Day long weekend. They were trying to match up John and me to go on the trip. I politely explained that I could not go, as it would be too dangerous with me being on crutches. John said, "Don't worry. I'll look after you." I wasn't convinced it was a good idea, but as we talked I became more comfortable with this guy. He was quiet but confident and had the most beautiful blue eyes. They were soft and honest. I trusted him instinctively.

To prepare for the trip we drove to the home of John's brother, Doug, in Port Elgin. The logistics of getting five or six canoes and their passengers to the launch site upstream, and to leave the vehicles downstream, was interesting. It reminded me of the riddle: How do you get a fox, a chicken, and a bag of seed across the river if you only have one boat? (I hope you know the answer because I'm not going through the details here). I had never done this before and I was impressed by the expertise of this group of young outdoor adventurers. John lifted me into the front of his canoe and then handed me my crutches and our cooler. We had fried chicken, doughnuts and beer. The Saugeen River is winding and rocky with interesting landscape and old bridges around every corner.

It was a day-long canoe trip from where we launched to near the mouth of the Saugeen. The sun was warm and the canoes flowed casually through the water with frequent pauses to enjoy the scenery. The river has numerous areas of rocks and rapids that challenge the novice canoeist. John showed me how to tell the position of the hidden rocks by the way the current flowed over them. To my surprise, John was able to stand in the back of the canoe and steer around all of the elements in the rapids that were entangling and tipping the other canoes. My adrenalin was pumping. I was scared but excited. When other canoes tipped, we rescued floating beer cans. At the end of the journey every canoe in our group had tipped except ours. Every person was wet except us. John climbed out of the canoe to pull it ashore. But first he lifted me from the canoe and said, "You can't be the only one dry!" He gently lowered me into the water amid the laughter of the gang. I clung to his neck. I felt I was part of something whole. This man was my hero, and soon to be my soul mate. That canoe trip continued to be an annual event and often it was a two-day trip with camping on the river bank, building a fire to cook our dinner and breakfast, and getting drenched in the rain.

I was still on crutches that Christmas when John and I started to blend our families. John was a single dad with a ten-year-old daughter, Christine. He was divorced, with full custody and they lived with his mom and dad. John drove a gravel truck. I was still working in finance and decided I wanted a career with more security. I set my goal on a Certified Management Accountant (CMA) designation. The Society of Management Accountants offered part-time courses through correspondence, with exams written at the University of Waterloo. I began my first course, Introductory Accounting 111, in January 1985.

After Christmas, I had surgery to remove the plate from my femur so that the bone could finish mending. The steel plate inhibited full, dense bone growth. So, with the plate removed, I had to stay on crutches for a few months longer, while working full-time, studying part-time, nurturing two children, and trying to establish a new relationship with a wonderful man. Then, just before I was due to write my first exam, my left thigh began giving me considerable pain. X-rays in London did not detect any cracks so it was determined that I was experiencing muscle spasms. Muscle relaxants and Tylenol 3s did not help. Three days later I could not get off the couch to go to the bathroom. My sister brought me a basin to urinate in. The pain was unbearable, so she called an ambulance. The orthopedic surgeon on call in emergency declared that my hip was broken. It couldn't be. I told him it wasn't broken, and further explained the recent surgery to lengthen my leg. The fact that I'd just had an x-ray three days ago indicated I must have been experiencing a muscle spasm. He became annoyed, held both my legs together by the ankles, and said "LOOK!" My left thigh was bent outward like a boomerang and my left leg was clearly inches shorter than my right leg. Reality hit me like a brick. After a year on crutches the femur was broken again. I screamed "NOOOOO!"

That day was March 16, 1985. I was given a shot of Demerol and put in traction again. This new orthopedic surgeon was very competent. In his opinion, the process of bone lengthening was premature and should not have been done. He planned to stabilize the lengthened bone in traction and then apply a body cast until it mended. This meant I would be in the hospital for months and not be able to sit for my first accounting exam. What else could go wrong?

Mom was looking after my children. She also spoke to my boss, Al Graff, about my predicament and the emotional strain it was causing me. Mr. Graff said not to worry about my job. It would be there when I came back. He also had connections with the Society of Management Accountants. He was able to arrange for a senior CMA member to bring a copy of the exam to my hospital room at the exact time other students were writing. That proctor sat with me during the allotted hours to testify that I wrote it legitimately. I will always be grateful for the support I received from Al Graff at that pivotal time in my life. I passed the exam and began studying for my next course while I lay in the hospital. I had plenty of time to study.

John visited me every day for three months. He brought me strawberry milkshakes and chocolate bars. Even when there was nothing to talk about, he just sat there beside me. Still I thought I would go insane. Being in traction I had to lie on my back in one position, without sitting up or rolling over for almost three months. I had a psychiatrist visit me and teach me meditation. He said it was a good sign that I thought I was going crazy. It meant I wasn't. If I was going crazy I wouldn't know it. I relied on that logic many times after that.

My Aunt Lois, who is my father's sister, came to visit me. We reconnected and I am grateful for that. It gave me the opportunity to meet my father again, years later, at my Grandpa McKone's funeral. When he saw me he said, "I'd know those eyes anywhere." That meant more to me than anyone could understand. I remember those words when I think of him.

When the day came that the body cast was placed on me, I was claustrophobic. I felt that I couldn't breathe. It was like being in a coffin and I begged to have it off. The doctor warned me that to remove it and place a pin in the bone would require another two surgeries and would be very risky. I could lose my leg. I chose to take the risk.

Not until June did I finally get released from the hospital with a steel pin in my femur and crutches under my arm, again. I don't remember how long I was on crutches that time. Then a year later I had to go back and have the pin removed from the bone. It's all over now. However, I am disappointed that my spine is still curved and I still walk with a limp. My hips are uneven and my knees are uneven. My left leg is longer from the hip to the knee, and shorter from the knee to the ankle, than my right leg. As a result, my balance is not good and it's worse on uneven surfaces and slopes. This is my cross to bear. The entire two years of surgery and crutches was for naught... except that I discovered my soul mate through it all.

Chapter 18

Keep Calm and Carry On

When I was no longer on crutches John and I used our rare vacation time together to travel. Our first family vacation was to Niagara Falls. We found that with three pre-teens in the back seat of the car, and only two windows, one of them is going to get a nosebleed. It was Adam. All hell broke loose when the girls freaked over getting Adam's blood on them. John pulled over at the first highway rest stop. With a wad of Kleenex over Adam's face, and his head tilted back, I walked him to the entrance between the men's washroom and the ladies' washroom. I pulled one way and Adam pulled the other way. Adam, 11 years old, would not go through the ladies' door, and I would not go through the men's door. I had to let go of the Kleenex and his nose and let go of him. My baby was growing up.

We didn't want any of the three kids to think their feelings were being neglected on this first bonding trip, but the three of them couldn't agree on a restaurant, or a hotel, or who got which bed. Tina was the eldest at the tender age of 13 and was expected to be more mature. Adam was the youngest, and the only boy, and always had to take the cot. Christine was only two months older than Adam, but had been an only child up until now, and perhaps felt like the odd person out. We wanted a pleasant trip for them all, but that was not going to be easy. Blending two families with children was a lot more challenging than we had imagined.

The next time John and I went to Niagara Falls, it was for a romantic weekend alone. We had dinner in the Revolving Dining Room, atop of the 520 foot Skylon Tower. I wore a sheer black spaghetti strap cocktail dress with a full twirling skirt. John was so handsome in a suit. The restaurant rotated slowly for a 360-degree view while dining. The outer ring of tables next to the windows was full of patrons. The inner ring of tables, where we were seated, was on an elevated platform to give a clear view over the window tables. We were cautioned about the step up from the aisle to the table. You know where this story is going. We had a wonderful romantic dinner. A few glasses of wine and I forgot all about the step.

"Are you ready to go?" John asked me with a twinkle in his eye.

"Yes, let's," I replied shyly.

Standing up and straightening my dress I took one step toward the aisle and went down, flying across the window table. The astonished diners helped me to my feet, along with John and the waiters. I apologized profusely. They were only concerned that I wasn't hurt. Luckily there were only empty dessert plates and beverages on their table. I offered to pay for their spilled beverages but they wouldn't hear of it. I couldn't think straight. I was shaken and embarrassed and needed some air. There was a nearby glass door where one could exit the dining room to the outdoor Observation Deck. I thought this would be a good idea to calm me down. It was a clear, starry night. We had just stepped outside and the wind blew my light swirly skirt up over my head so I couldn't see a thing. But everyone inside could see everything. It was not sexy like Marilyn Monroe in the white dress scene. It was comic relief for the diners watching through the glass walls. John guided me back inside and we went straight for the elevator, with our heads looking down at the floor, and then drove back to our room. That was enough excitement for one night.

Our next romantic trip was a drive to Quebec City over Christmas holidays. We stayed in the historic Chateau Frontenac in Old Quebec. Our room was small and ordinary, but the architecture, the lobby, and the dining room were large and elegant. There were multiple sets of elevators in the lobby that looked as if they were made of shiny gold. I was so captivated by the gold elevators that I wanted to get a marvelous photo of them. It was annoying that a group of men were standing in front of them. John tried to motion me to get on the elevator, but I wouldn't leave until these guys dispersed so I could get a photo of the elevators. I finally did, but was still complaining about it as we rode in an elevator up to our room with two of the last guys. Once we were alone John told me those guys were the Montreal Canadiens hockey team, and so were the guys in the elevator with us. I didn't recognise them in suits rather than red jerseys. I wish I would have known. I could have taken photos of them with the elevators. He didn't tell me because he didn't want me to act like a tourist and embarrass him.

My Grandma McKone gave me an early inheritance of $1000 before she went into a nursing home. I was very honoured to receive that from her. I chose to spend it on a Disneyworld vacation with our blended family when the kids were 13 to 15. It was a little easier than the Niagara trip, but Adam still got the cot in the living room and the girls were still full of drama. I have never regretted any trip we have taken or any new experience. I have learned something from them all, good or bad.

Chapter 19

The 6th Configuration: New Family Dynamics

Christmas 1985 surprised both Mom and I with diamond engagement proposals. Paul asked Mom to marry him and John asked me to be his wife. In 1986, John and I bought a house together on Church Street, and Mom moved in with Paul. Alison was attending medical college and dating Vic, who we all adored. I was working full-time for Chrysler and still taking management accounting courses to enhance my career.

After each three-month course, I wrote an exam at the University of Waterloo. On my way to my 10th exam, "Taxation" in 1988, my car broke down. Again, in the middle of nowhere, on a country road outside of Waterloo, the engine went BANG and the car slowed to a stop. Later, I discovered it ran out of oil and the piston went through the engine wall (or something like that). I saw a couple of farm houses down the road. I thought I would walk to one of them, phone John, and ask him what to do. The first farm house had no cars around and a barking dog outside the door. I wasn't going near there. The second farm was a long way up the road and had a very long laneway. It was December and I was trudging through snow. Before I got to the laneway I heard a pickup truck come along. There were two working men in the truck. They were heading to Waterloo and said they could drop me off at the university. Once again, I hesitated, but I knew if I didn't take this ride I would miss my exam and have to do the course again. Against better judgement I climbed in the truck between the two guys. They turned out to be pleasant and worked for a company that made solariums. They gave me a brochure and ever since then I have wanted to add a solarium to the sunny side of my house.

I made it to my exam in time to write, but to my dismay I had left my taxation text book in the broken car, and this was an open-book exam. I had to write the exam without reference material, but that may have saved the day. I am a slow reader. It's possible that I would have wasted too much time looking up references. I finished the exam from what memory I could muster, and a little logical guessing, and got a "B" grade. That was good enough. I had previously received scholarships for highest marks in both "Organizational Behaviour" and "Economics." Although a slow reader, I used to have a very good retention of information.

After the exam, John came to my rescue as he always has. The next day Mom and I went to the Chrysler dealer and I picked out a car on the lot and bought it. I needed a car for work. It made sense to me since I got a discount for working for the company. John called me at work that afternoon and said we should go out and look for a new motor. I told him we didn't need to because I had bought a car at lunch time. I thought he'd be proud of me. He dropped the phone… then he really lost it on me. He hollered something about "How could I do that without consulting him?" We discussed it later that evening. The fact that it was such a big deal to him was a surprise to me. I had been independent for too long. Now I understand that men and women shop for cars differently.

During those years of working, studying, and raising three teenagers, John and I had different parenting skills. We tried to be fair to all of them without raising entitled brats. In hindsight, there were situations that I wish I would have handled differently. Christine and Adam were 12 and Tina was 14 when we bought a house together. Each child had their own room. In April 1988, John and I were married. Our children, my sister and John's brother were our witnesses. Shortly after that things really changed. Christine, now 14, was taking more liberties and heading down a dangerous path. I encouraged John to be more strict and that failed. I didn't want to be the mean step-mother. Tina thought it unfair that she was older and had fewer liberties than Christine. I made some ridiculous rules trying to settle quarrels. Without going into details, matters got worse and a counsellor recommended that Christine live with her mother for a while in Toronto. There were two advantages for her. Christine would be away from some peers who were a bad influence, and she would be in the family home of her mother, step-father, and three wee half-sisters who would be a good distraction for her. John agreed but resented the fact that my children were still living with us. Within a year, Adam, who was almost 16, asked if he could live with his father. It broke my heart. Adam was intelligent, involved in lots of extra-curricular activities, and loved church, confirmation, and several times performed the sermons at Zion Lutheran Church.

I drilled Adam about why he wanted to live with his dad. He could visit him anytime. I asked if he was having trouble with John. He said no. Adam insisted that he wanted to get to know his dad better since he would soon be going off to college. I was sure it had something to do with John and Christine's situation. I felt guilt and resentment in our home. Adam denied it. He said that he didn't want to hurt me, but he really wanted this opportunity. What could I say? I let him go, but it really hurt. There was still tension between John and me. John's mother inflamed the situation. She hated to see Christine go to Toronto. Christine visited us often and over the years she grew into a lovely young lady, wife, and mother that we are proud of. As time went by John and Tina grew closer, especially after he got her a summer job working on his construction crew. She developed a new respect for him and vice-versa.

As for Adam, sometime after he turned 16 he got a part-time job pumping gas, moved out of his dad's home, rented a place with some friends, and missed a lot of school. Despite his high grades, it took him seven years to complete high school due to his poor attendance record. For about two of those years he and I were estranged. I could not condone his lifestyle. Trying to do the right thing raising children is very difficult. I was fortunate that Mom, Tina and Alison continued to keep in touch with him. During this time, he wrote music and poems to express his feelings. I still have copies of his writings. They are in my keepsake box.

While we were estranged, Adam was living with friends in shared apartments around Stratford. At one point, he and his friend Rick rented a place on Erie Street. They were soon joined by another friend, Pattie, whom Adam had briefly dated. Before long, they traded their downstairs apartment for a larger one upstairs and invited a fourth friend, Chuck, to share expenses.

The place was abuzz with a steady stream of visitors and frequent parties. The procession of guests who would come to hang out included Jeremy Bieber — Chuck's former roommate and Pattie's ex-boyfriend — whom she'd eventually hook up with again, long after everyone had moved out of the Erie Street loft.

There's a reason I put this tidbit in my story. When Adam finally graduated high school a couple of years later, he attended Concordia University in Montreal, and dropped in to see Pattie on one of his first visits home. Now a single mother, she introduced him to her baby boy, Justin. A couple of years later they spoke on the phone, with Pattie raving about her toddler's musical genius and Adam accepting this as typical mother's pride. He couldn't have known then just how right Pattie was — or how wrong —depending your opinion of her son, Justin's, music.

In an effort to heal our relationship, I arranged for a hot air balloon ride for Tina, Adam, and me for Adam's 19th birthday in 1993. It was the beginning of a renewed bond for the rest of our lives. I now believe that Adam needed that time to experiment, learn life lessons, and find himself, the way so many teenagers need to do before they mature.

On the other hand, Tina was never a problem. She was mature beyond her years. Perhaps she tried too hard. Tina had a lot of responsibility being the eldest child of divorced parents. When Tina was 19 she became aware she had Obsessive-Compulsive Disorder. Her doctor said that she might consider a mild medication to balance chemicals in her brain. To my knowledge she refused to take any medication. She manages her compulsion for perfectionism quite well, but it sometimes creates conflict between us.

Chapter 20

The 7th Configuration: Shakespeare

Tina, John and I moved from Stratford to a unique A-frame house in the village of Shakespeare. Tina was in Grade 13, her final year living with us full-time. We had extra bedrooms set up for each of Christine and Adam when they came home to visit. John was still playing ball and was treasurer of the Shakespeare Optimists. I left my job at Chrysler for career advancement at Allied Signal. I joined Beta Sigma Phi Sorority and it enriched my life. I was also still taking three CMA courses a year. Our life was full with friends and family.

Alison and Vic had announced their engagement, and the wedding was set for July 13, 1991. I would be her Matron of Honour. Tina was a bridesmaid and Adam was an usher. It was a beautiful wedding. Vic is a beloved brother, and eventually their four children would complete our family. My godson Joel was born in 1993, my niece Nicole (Niki) in 1995, Chad in 2001, and Ben in 2003. They are all important to me.

In 1992, I changed jobs again to expand my accounting experience in anticipation of graduating. I failed the final exam on my first attempt. After studying for seven years and achieving 18 credits, I was dejected and ready to give up. It was the last exam to be offered under the old qualification process because the new process was upgraded. I would have to write an entrance exam to qualify for the new two-year Professional Development Program. After that I would have to write another final exam.

I had just started a new job at Fischer Aktiengesellschaft (FAG Bearings) and I blamed that for my poor performance on the exam. In reality, I just wasn't ready for it. My new boss, Karl Angler, boosted my confidence and encouraged me to keep at it. I wrote the new program's entrance exam in 1993 and graduated in 1995 as a CMA. It was the first graduation ceremony that I had ever attended for myself, and it was an outstanding formal event. The two years of professional development lectures and projects were invaluable to my career. They gave me confidence, experience, and coping skills that I would not have had if I had passed the first exam in 1992. This is another example of the fact that everything happens for a reason, and every dark cloud has a silver lining.

Chapter 21

Diane Lyoness, CMA

When I began as Cost Accountant at FAG in 1992 the company was just launching SAP (System Applications and Products), IBM's leading enterprise resource planning software. Throughout my career, I became proficient with the Financial Accounting and Controlling Modules of SAP and their relationship to the Sales, Production, and Inventory modules. As such, I was able to help troubleshoot and problem solve with my associates in all departments of the company and become a valuable asset.

FAG was a good fit for me. I bonded with co-workers and had respect and admiration for my manager. Karl encouraged me to get involved with upper management and take visiting VIPs out to dinner on behalf of the company. This was a whole new level of responsibility for me. My first dinner engagement was to take an SAP consultant, Michael Volker, from Germany to dinner at a posh restaurant in St. Jacobs. Before entering the restaurant, I caught my high heel in a sidewalk grate. I had to step out of my shoe and Michael got down on his knees in order to pull it out of the grate. I was so embarrassed. Then between courses I had a coughing spell and excused myself to the ladies' room. That broke the ice. Michael and I became great friends and consulted one another often. He once told Karl that "Diane could find a needle in a haystack."

In early 1995 John left his job on road construction and joined the water-pump bearing team at FAG. I was offered the opportunity to be controller for the Automotive Division at FAG in Joplin, Missouri. I would still be reporting to Karl Angler in Stratford. In August 1996, John and I sold our house in Shakespeare and moved to the centre of the United States on Route 66.

Chapter 22

The 8th Configuration: Joplin, MO

We were in Joplin only two weeks when I got word that my mother had lung cancer. There I was, living 1500 kilometres away, leaving Alison with the burden of Mom's healthcare. Thankfully, as an ultrasound tech, Alison had the knowledge and contacts to help her. At first, we thought the cancer was confined to the lining of her lung. Next, we found out one lung might need to be removed. Then we found it had spread beyond the lung and she would need chemo. I went home for Thanksgiving and Mom looked frail. Alison was trying everything that might help prolong her life, like shark cartilage and barley green supplements.

We were waiting to hear of a date for chemo to start. A doctor friend of Alison's mentioned a cancer clinic in Mexico with amazing results. In the middle of November, Alison put Mom on a plane (with wheelchair and oxygen tank) and I left Joplin and met her plane in San Diego. Then we went by ambulance to Tijuana. Mom and I had a double room. I had permission from FAG for a two-week leave and I took work with me.

Mom was on a special regimen of diet, herbs, coffee enemas, and psychological and emotional therapy. It seemed to be helping for a few days. Then she felt the need to write letters to all the people she loved, and needed closure with. After that she went downhill to the point where I knew she would not be allowed on a public airplane. I feared she would die in Mexico. In the middle of the night, in a panic, I ordered transportation to the San Diego airport and a Lear jet ambulance to London, Ontario.

Alison met me at the London airport with an ambulance that took her to Victoria Hospital. For two days she was lucid. The third morning we went in to see her sitting up in a chair with her breakfast tray in front of her. She leered at us but never spoke. When asked what was wrong, she took her coffee cup in one hand and her milk glass in the other, and flung them at each of us.

What a shock! A nurse came to help and comfort us and explain that this was the illness taking over. Later that day she went into a coma that she never came out of. Tina arrived from Toronto and together Tina, Alison and I stayed with her for three days. We slept in chairs, on cots in the hall, or in a corner curled up on the tread of a treadmill. No one asked us to leave, which was kind. She passed away on November 29, 1996. It was ten years to the month after her beloved Paul passed away from a sudden heart attack.

Ironically, Mom's mom (Granny Roth who gave me the beer many years ago) passed away earlier that same month, November 3, 1996. She died of natural causes at the age of 100 years and 1 month. She took my mom with her way too soon. Mom was only 64. I heard relatives say, "Granny wouldn't go without Patty." They left us the same month. We all miss Mom every day.

It was difficult leaving my family after that and going back to Joplin to a new job, but I had made the commitment. Thank God I had the support of John by my side. It was another year before John was able to get a visa to work in Joplin. His job there was building and maintaining machine interconnects. John is a natural builder. He can think through the construction or repair of anything.

My responsibilities were planning and controlling the Automotive Division, and financial reporting to Stratford, Ontario; Danbury, Connecticut; and Schweinfurt, Germany. Danbury was the legal entity head office for the United States subsidiaries of FAG. Stratford was the head office for Canada and the North American Automotive Division.

Tom Strouss was my right-hand man and cost accountant. He and I had plenty of travel opportunities to Stratford, Boston, Danbury, New York, Detroit, and of course Germany. While in America, John and I had the opportunity to vacation in Texas (with Adam), Arkansas, Yellowstone

National Park, and Hawaii. We had a three-bedroom house and loved to entertain friends and family from Canada. Several co-workers from Stratford were also contracted to Joplin for periods of time. Murray and Barb Meadows, and Rick and Jan Smith come to mind when I think of the parties we had in Joplin. I must mention Linda and David Shultz, our best friends from Joplin. We met them when we first arrived. Linda is a giver — a wonderful friend who would do anything for you. We kept in touch by email for years afterwards.

Chapter 23

The 9th Configuration: Benmiller

The corporate strategy was for me to return to Canada from Joplin in three years and the timing was perfect. It just so happened in 1999 that John and I became grandparents in March and moved back to Stratford in October. John's daughter Christine, and Don Lush from Toronto, had a baby boy named Austin. We didn't get to Toronto to see them as much as we would have liked. When we returned to Canada we rented a townhouse in Stratford for a year, while we were building our dream house on five acres of woodland on the Maitland River in Benmiller, near Goderich. Travelling between Stratford and Goderich on a regular basis left little time for anything else.

John is a professional with a chainsaw. Together we cleared the trees for a winding driveway through the woods to build our house with a view of the river. It was a labour of love. We moved in October, 2000. Our first Christmas was spectacular with family, friends, co-workers, and beautiful white snowflakes. I decorated the house with natural cedar boughs and small white birch logs. We had in-floor heating and a natural stone fireplace. However, the two heat sources did not work well together to provide even heating. When the fireplace was glowing, the house got too hot and the floor heat went off. When the fire went down, it took forever for the floor to heat the room again. Now we know what not to do if we build again.

We loved living in Benmiller even though the drive to work in Stratford was an hour each way. John returned to FAG in the Machine Maintenance department. My new position was Special Projects Manager including managing the financial reporting for Joplin. This put me on the executive payroll, which was a nice bonus. There were plenty of projects to keep me busy. Many of these required trips to Germany for SAP upgrades and new product launches.

In early 2001, FAG needed a controller in Debrecen, Hungary and Karl asked me to consider it. I agreed to fill in for three months until they found a permanent replacement. I was on the plane in February, just four months after moving to our new home.

I flew to Budapest, rented a car and drove three hours to Debrecen, near the border to Romania. At that time, Hungary was not in the European Union and it had only been ten years since communist control ended. Most people in stores and restaurants spoke no English and about 5% spoke German. I knew a little German but I was lost immediately. The Hungarian alphabet has more letters than ours. Many of their words and names of streets and towns have 20 or more characters, some of which I couldn't pronounce. I felt at times like I was on another planet. It was only by the grace of God that I found the place I was to stay on the first night.

The plant secretary, Elizabeth, was Ukrainian and she spoke English. The human resources supervisor spoke English quite well. I knew the plant manager. He was from Brazil and had worked in Stratford briefly. I tried to learn Hungarian in all my spare time. It is a difficult language that is similar to Russian. I had the most unexpected problems outside the office. Trying to buy a few groceries was a challenge. Most brands were strange and the labels had no English. Their currency was Forints. One Canadian dollar was worth about 200 Forints. I was so lost!

On weekends, I tried to see some of the country and Elizabeth was a great help. She showed me things I'd never seen before like a stork's nest on top of a chimney or on a hydro pole. The nest was large enough for a human to curl up in. We went to a horse farm where there happened to be a movie crew filming a documentary about Hungarian cowboys trick riding. They wore ruffled shirts, long colourful skirts to their boots, and sombrero-type hats.

They rode bareback and stood upon the horses' backs as they were galloping in circles. They even jumped from horse to horse while in motion. When the filming stopped we went up to talk to the cowboys. I didn't know what the conversation was about. Elizabeth turned to me and asked if I would like a ride. I love horses and I rode as a child. I'll try anything once. Of course, I said, "Sure." The horse was huge. Two cowboys helped me up onto it, behind the rider. I did not expect to be riding tandem. There was no saddle and no stirrups for my feet, and nothing for me to hold onto except the back of the man in front of me. He took off trotting and I almost bounced off. Then he went faster and faster. I feared for my life. The rider was rather fat and I could not get my arms around his waist. I felt myself slipping right and left. My feet couldn't even grip this huge horse around the belly. I kept yelling "STOP!" but he never responded. In my mind, I saw myself falling under its feet. Finally it stopped. I wanted to slap the rider but I didn't. I was so shaken up I could hardly breathe. Elizabeth smiled and said she wished she'd had a camera.

Learning food words on a menu was a priority. I translated and ordered tomato salad and beer. I was brought a side plate of sliced tomatoes. Often when I spoke my order in either Hungarian or German I noticed other customers and staff giggling and staring at me. This can be very unsettling when one is alone.

Halfway through my term John came to visit me. I met him in Budapest (and got a speeding ticket on the way). We spent a couple of nights there. Dinner one evening at a fine authentic restaurant was lovely. There was a musical trio playing violins and accordion. There were Hungarian dancers in colourful costumes. The wine was delicious. When it came time to pay I offered my credit card but they wanted cash. I did not have enough cash on me. My effort to figure this out at our table was embarrassing. I understood that one of us had to stay at the table and one had to go to the ATM at the police station down the street to get cash.

It was after 9 p.m., dark, and I had to walk alone in downtown Budapest. When I got to the police station it appeared to be closed. The ATM was outside the building. There was a small group of teens standing on the sidewalk between me and the ATM. This did not look like a good idea to me. Without an alternative, I walked past them to the ATM, withdrew the money, and walked past them again without breathing. I knew they were watching me as I walked away and eventually I ran.

John and I visited the beautiful historical buildings, castles, and parks in Budapest and then went to my place in Debrecen for a few days. Thermal baths are a big thing in Hungary. Many Germans vacation there to use the spa bath houses. They have numerous indoor pools with varying temperatures of therapeutic waters. We also drove to visit our FAG plant in Austria and spent a few days in the beautiful city of Vienna. The week went fast. John went home and I was alone again.

At the end of my three months, corporate office insisted I stay longer. I politely declined on the grounds I was guaranteed I could return home. I knew this could be career suicide. My daughter was getting married in five months. To support her and be part of her marriage preparations was the most important thing to me.

Chapter 24

Tina and JD get Married

Tina met John David Maxwell Ross at high school in 1988. They dated off and on until Tina's third year at OCAD in Toronto. That's when JD finished his university degree. They rented an apartment in Toronto and have been together ever since. JD was the 1990 high school valedictorian and was one of ten Canada Scholars that year. As I said earlier, he came into my store to get candy when he was a little boy. It's a small world.

I loved JD like a son from the very start. Before I moved to Joplin in 1996, he took me aside and promised he would take good care of Tina, and that he planned to ask her to marry him one day. That pleased and comforted me when I was so far from her. Shortly after I moved to Joplin we discovered Mom had cancer. While I was with Mom in the cancer clinic in Mexico I confided in her what JD had told me. She was so pleased. Two weeks later she passed away, knowing that her children and grandchildren were all in good hands.

JD and Tina had a long engagement and were married on September 22, 2001. Eleven days earlier, New York's twin towers were destroyed and all hell broke loose. There were some very nervous moments wondering what would happen next, and how it might impact the wedding.

As it turned out, they had a beautiful outdoor garden wedding on a farm near Hamilton. JD was handsome in his Scottish Ross dress tartan and Tina was his beautiful princess. It poured rain the night before. On their wedding day, the sun shone bright and the world was clean, green, and beautiful. Tina walked down the bridal path to the sweet music of a harp. They were united and strolled off arm in arm, following a Scottish bagpiper, to their reception hall. Their wedding brought all their parents together in unison and support for them.

JD and Tina lived in a sweet little cottage in Oakville, Ontario. JD managed an auto leasing company and Tina was a graphic designer. She obtained her first position immediately upon graduating and worked her way up the ladder to become the senior designer for Pigeon Branding & Design. Her clients were some of the biggest names in beer, cigarettes and household products. I still have mementos from her advertising and packaging campaign for Tim Hortons' 40th Anniversary. She could never talk to me about what she was working on because it was all top secret until the products were launched. I am so proud of her creative talents.

Chapter 25

Adam Goes to Japan

A few months after Tina was married, Adam had surgery for an acid reflux problem, for which he had been taking medication since he was 12 years old. He had just graduated from Concordia University. That December he had surgery on his esophagus, and afterwards was having huge problems trying to swallow anything to sustain him. I brought him home from Montreal to help him heal, as he was in a lot of pain. Something wasn't right. Alison knew a surgeon in London. With her connections, Adam was treated by a knowledgeable surgeon, when others seemed to not know what was wrong. Alison's career in medicine has been a gift from God to every member of my family at one time or another.

Adam stayed with us in Benmiller for most of 2002. He had a contract job as a writer for the Goderich Signal Star news. By the end of summer, he was approved to take a position as an English teacher in Japan through the Japan Exchange and Teaching Programme (JET). Adam was placed in a little village called Tanto-cho, in the prefecture of Hyogo, near Osaka, Japan. There he taught English to Grade 7, 8, and 9 students for three years.

I still have Adam's emails from his first year in Japan. He was faced with adapting to the strict standards of the Japanese culture. It was no use pleading his case with logical arguments. For example, Adam wanted to rollerblade in the village, but this was not allowed. He took his case to the local police who said it wasn't safe. They listened to Adam's arguments. Cars were allowed to drive in the dark without headlights. The rain gutters were three feet deep between the road and the sidewalk, and a person or bike could easily fall in them. The police agreed that yes that was unsafe but that's the way it is. He explained his own high safety standards when rollerblading. They nodded in agreement. So, is it OK? No, that is not allowed. No explanation necessary.

Another example of Adam's frustration was with the school where he taught. Japan is not as cold as Canada but it does get snow at times. On a snow day, the kids stay home but the teachers go to school and shovel the parking lot. All the teachers line up at one end of the lot. The person at the far left passes a shovelful of snow to the right. Each one passes it to the right end of the line and they all take one step forward. Adam found this tedious. He is a tall man from Canada and very good at shovelling snow. He showed them that he could take a large sweeping shovelful and clear an area on his own faster. That was not acceptable. This is how we do it. You have to fall in line and do it this way with us.

Adam, who had been a great debater in high school, and could argue that black is white, had to learn to accept without question or compromise. Over the first three years I saw Adam mellowing in understanding and acceptance of another's culture. Adam has a great sense of humour and I am proud of the man he is today.

In 2003, John and I went to Japan to visit Adam. He had been there for only one year and was overjoyed to show us all the unique places he had found and the wonderful people he had met. It really was quite an experience. John and I stayed in a home for the elderly. There was a spare section for visitors to stay and it was very low cost. We slept on an authentic tatami mat. The bathroom had a hole in the tile floor where you crouch and drop your waste, then hose it down if you miss the hole. Every house has slippers at the door for each guest, and different slippers to wear in the bathroom, for obvious reasons.

The cherry blossoms and tulip gardens were in bloom when we were there in April. Tanto-cho is a small farming community. Only the young children, their mothers, and the very old still live there. From Grade 10 onwards, most young people go to the big cities to finish their education and do not return to the smaller villages. After three years with the JET Programme, instead of coming back to Canada, Adam was hired to teach English and French in a private school called Vanilla City.

Now, more than a decade later, Adam is still in Japan. He manages an online English learning program, and teaches English classes for various schools and companies. Adam has been with his partner, Shinobu, since 2004. She is a nurse and a fabulous cook. Together they have operated their own international restaurant, called "The Stix", in Toyooka. Now they live in the outlying village of Kehi, by the Sea of Japan. John and I were back to visit them in 2013 and I hope one day to take Tina and her daughters for an amazing experience there.

Chapter 26

9/11 Shook Our world

September 11, 2001 is a date that changed everyone's world in some way. The terrorist attack that began with New York's twin towers is still inspiring fear and paranoia in every country of the world today. That entire week was momentous in my life.

On Monday, September 10, I went into work at FAG in Stratford to begin training accounting staff for a new and major SAP upgrade. A young girl from SAP Germany was assisting with the nuances. As soon as I arrived I was told that a private German company called Schaeffler had initiated a hostile takeover of our company. Very soon we would know what the implications would be, but for now we would proceed with the SAP upgrade project that I had trained for over the past six months. It was difficult to concentrate on the project with everyone talking about this news and new management speculation.

On Tuesday, September 11, we were in training in an on-site classroom and interrupted by the news of the first plane crashing into the tower in New York. While mulling that over, the second plane crashed, and so on. Before the end of the day airports were shut down and rumours of terror all over the world were rampant. I was responsible for the young girl from Germany who had never been out of her country until three days before. She was afraid she wouldn't get home at the end of the week. To make matters worse she got word that her mother was taken to hospital with heart problems over worry about her daughter here in North America.

Everyone was scrambling to understand what was happening and how it would impact their lives. Everyone was afraid. No one could concentrate on work. Tina's wedding was in less than two weeks. What if there were more attacks to come?

On Wednesday, September 12, my boss, Karl, requested he and I have a lunch meeting off-site. He informed me that on his return from a business trip the previous week he had been in a New York airport two days before the attack and missed his plane. Rather than wait until the next day he had rented a car and driven home. Why was he in New York? It was extremely confidential. He had taken a detour for a job interview with another major company. It appeared the ball was in his court if he wanted the position.

I was completely shocked. Karl was vice president and had been with FAG for twenty-some years... since leaving school. He was a loyal and dedicated employee. I had no idea he was even looking.

The timing of his recent interview, with the announcement of the hostile takeover of FAG, combined to encourage him to seriously consider it. He confidentially discussed some of the pros and cons with me. What did I think of it? Karl was looking for opinions and was concerned about uprooting his family.

With my track record, I encouraged him to take it. The position was with STIHL Inc., a manufacturer of power tools in Virginia Beach, Virginia. STIHL was also German and family-owned. The USA subsidiary in Virginia Beach had grown larger than the parent company in Waiblingen, Germany. The position was Vice President of Finance and Administration and the company was expanding their use of SAP.

So, there it was. In the past year, John and I had built our dream house by a river in the woods, one hour from where we worked. Since then I had spent months working in Hungary and several weeks working in Germany, while super-excited about my daughter's upcoming wedding. I had been trying to focus on the details of our SAP upgrade, and figure out how we could adapt it to FAG's needs. Now in a matter of three days I had learned how a huge company can be changed overnight without notice. I had seen how the lives of people around the world could change in a day of terror. I had been privy to a secret that would change my entire work environment as I knew it, and I could watch it all unfold. That was really overwhelming.

PART IV

Chapter 27

The 10th Configuration: Virginia

I no longer remember when Karl formerly announced his resignation. I think it was in the early part of 2002. He gave at least three months' notice, maybe more. I really didn't know a single person who didn't like Karl, so there was a lot of sadness and a lot of tears around the various good-bye parties that people held. I knew he would keep in touch with many of his supporters by email.

In the summer of 2002 I received a phone call. I remember it well because I was at home exercising on my elliptical trainer. John answered the phone, "It's for you. It's Karl." After the usual pleasantries he asked, "Would you and John consider moving to Virginia Beach? I have a job that would be perfect for you. It's a piece of cake and good money, too. SAP Project Manager."

I was really excited about the prospects of a new experience, but would need more details to discuss the opportunity with John. We left it that Karl would call back in a week or so. John and I both had misgivings about leaving the country again after building our dream home. I half hoped Karl would make me a fantastic offer that was too good to refuse. Then I didn't hear from him for a month. Wondering what kind of game he was playing I called him. He said the position he had in mind was filled by a young lad from STIHL Germany that was being transferred to the USA for a year.

Karl thought I didn't sound interested enough on the phone. He suggested I might consider taking the position next year when the ex-pat returned to Germany. I was disappointed but I convinced myself that it was for the best. Maybe we wouldn't move at all.

In early 2003, Karl invited John and me to Virginia Beach to scope out the area and for me to have an interview with some of the managers that I might be working with. The interviews went very well. We were extremely impressed with the STIHL production and administration facilities. Both the company and the position would be a move upward on the career ladder. Most of all we loved the ocean, the wide sandy beaches, the three-mile boardwalk, the seafood restaurants, and the warm, sunny climate.

Next, we negotiated compensation packages. STIHL would apply for green cards for both John and I to live and work in USA. The process could take a year to complete. Until then I had a working visa but John could not work in the USA. So, my US salary in Canadian dollars had to exceed what John and I were currently earning combined. At that time, the US dollar was worth $1.50 Canadian and we worked out an equitable package.

As for FAG, much had changed since Schaeffler had taken over. The Canadian company lost its autonomy and became just a plant of the American head office. The working climate had deteriorated since Karl had left. I wasn't very happy there anymore and Virginia Beach looked pretty welcoming. In June 2003, John and I both gave FAG notice and started packing.

We were going to sell our home in Benmiller and then changed our mind. John's parents agreed to move in and live there while we were in Virginia. That way we would have a familiar place to stay when we came home to visit and we would likely retire there someday. By that time, John's parents would be ready for a retirement community. It was a symbiotic relationship.

The moving truck loaded up everything we owned including my car. John packed our personal effects in his Jeep and we headed east to Boston and then south along the east coast from Cape Cod to Virginia.

A four-bedroom house with a red brick facade on Indian River Road was where we parked ourselves for the first two years. We had plenty of room for visitors from Canada. We couldn't have a vegetable garden because the land was clay and the summers were too hot and dry. We were only there two months when Hurricane Isabel came ashore in September 2003. We headed for West Virginia for two days. Upon return, our house was intact but we had no electricity for a week. Many areas were not so lucky. After that experience, we bought a generator and have never needed it since.

My first year working at STIHL was not as pleasant as I had hoped. I had my 50th birthday just days before we moved. The age didn't bother me — turning 30 bothered me — but I was surprised to find that most of the office staff were age 20 to 35. I never before considered age differences to matter, but after the first month in this new work environment I was feeling old and inadequate. I already knew what it felt like to be the new kid on the block. It was no surprise that people were suspicious at first and were polite, but cold. I expected that. However, very few of them warmed up over time. The girls I worked most closely with did not.

The way in which STIHL used SAP systems was entirely different from FAG. Karl found that as well and that's why he thought I could help him out. In addition, I was not familiar with the auxiliary systems that STIHL used to feed data into SAP. I discovered that I could not learn new methods as quickly as I used to. I had worked with the systems and the people at FAG for 10 years.

In familiarizing myself with this alternate work environment I had a lot of questions. These young people at STIHL were not very helpful in showing, telling and sharing information. I know that one or two girls were trying to sabotage my projects.

It took about a year for me to realize why some of the girls were keeping me at a distance: it was fear. Karl Angler had only been Vice President at STIHL for a year and had already implemented several changes in processes. People don't favour change. Now he'd brought in a person he'd favoured from his past, and from Canada, moreover. Many Americans were not fond of Canadians at that time. He put me in a position to implement new projects that would affect information technology, cost accounting and financial accounting. They clearly felt threatened and I was not welcome.

Two ladies who were my age did not feel threatened. Karen and Cheryl were great friends and made my job enjoyable. Gradually others came on board. I may have been slow at the start but I did prove myself several times by tackling problems and then implementing solutions to make other people's jobs easier. I could see the bulb light up, "Oh, maybe she's not so bad after all."

John was not legally able to work in Virginia. He took on renovation projects and did all the home chores so that we could enjoy time together when I wasn't working. Strolling along the Atlantic Ocean boardwalk was a favourite pastime. We visited the Blue Ridge Mountains and Shenandoah River Valley. We vacationed in historic Charleston, South Carolina with John's parents. John joined me on a work trip to Stuttgart, Germany where he enjoyed the Mercedes-Benz Museum. We took a Holland America Cruise along the inside passage from Vancouver to Alaska. There we visited our friend Elizabeth, travelled to Denali National Park and saw Mt. McKinley. The highlight for John was fishing for halibut to take home.

In 2004, I had a car accident on my way to work and totaled my cougar. I was not hurt or charged, but I was lucky. I was making a right hand turn on a yellow light when a van sped through the intersection. In trying to avoid him, my cougar jumped the median. Fortunately, there was no traffic in the oncoming lanes.

Following that incident John found me VAL, a beautiful, red 2001 Ford Escape. She was purchased on Valentine's Day and she was a nice car. I had her until 2014 when I sold her to my sister.

Also in 2004, John's daughter Christine married Donny in Las Vegas. We flew there for the wedding and visited Hoover Dam. I pulled a rock out of the dam for a souvenir. We rented a convertible, but I would not recommend that. The desert sun is too hot to drive with the top down but we purchased a couple of hats and sweated profusely in our topless sports car.

Speaking of weddings, Karl's assistant Silya, a lovely young girl from Germany, married an American Naval Officer. John and I were invited to their 2006 wedding in Annapolis, Maryland. They had a traditional Naval Academy Chapel wedding, complete with the military sword arch ceremonial walk. It was very impressive and I was honoured to be there. Unfortunately, I was on crutches. I had twisted my left knee when a rogue wave took me out while swimming in the ocean a few weeks earlier. It was so unfortunate. It happened in August 2006 when Tina and JD came to visit us for a week. I am so thankful that Tina wasn't in the water at that time because she was six months pregnant with my first granddaughter.

Many of our sisters, brothers, cousins, parents, and kids visited us during our three years there. Our good friends Jean and John Edmonds came to visit. They hoped to see the Oceana Naval Air Show. Unfortunately, I got the dates mixed up and we missed the show but we had a good time anyway. We had met Jean and John on a recent trip to Costa Rica. Ever since then we have been great friends and travel companions.

Alison and Vic came once a year to the beach, their van packed with Joel, Niki, Chad, Ben and strollers, clothes, and beach paraphernalia. What a long drive for them. Mom would be smiling from heaven seeing us all together. One of my favourite pictures is the eight of us on the beach in Virginia. I have the best sister in the whole world. One time they even managed to stuff Adam in the van when they came to visit. I will never forget the morning all eight of them (including John) were crowding in the doorway waving good-bye as I was heading to work. Alison hollered, "Don't work too hard" and Adam hollered, "Work hard Mom, you've got a lot of hungry mouths to feed." We all laughed. It was a great way to start the day.

Virginia Beach is a sprawling coastal community that grew near Norfolk, at the mouth of Chesapeake Bay. Norfolk has the world's largest Naval Air base to protect Washington, DC from intruders via the Atlantic Ocean. There is much history there dating back to 1607. South of Virginia Beach is the state of North Carolina. It was near enough for a day trip. There are wide sandy beaches and cottages on stilts to protect them from tidal surges. One of the nearby coastal areas is Kitty Hawk, where the Wright brothers made the first controlled powered flight in 1903. Of course, there is a museum and tourist attractions, but what impressed me was the enormous sand dunes that seem to go on forever.

Chapter 28

Be Careful What You Wish For!

We had some medical issues while in Virginia. John was suspected of having hemochromatosis, which is an abnormal accumulation of iron in certain organs that can become toxic. His complexion was grey and he was generally feeling unwell. The treatment was to take blood high in iron from him, and reduce his intake of iron-rich foods. It was believed to be genetic. However, in Canada in later years that diagnosis was refuted for John. Medicine is not an exact science.

In 2005, I began getting what doctors called "cluster headaches" — sharp pains in the back of my head. I saw a neurologist and during the consultation he asked me unusual questions that led to exposing my history of having some unusual habits.

"Do you grunt?" he asked me.

I was taken aback! What kind of question is that? Then I thought about it and answered, "Of course not... but I used to when I was young."

As far back as I can remember I have had habits that I tried to hide from people. Now I have learned they were compulsive tics. It took me a long time to hold an egg without breaking it. I am still nervous holding a raw egg. From the age of four I had a difficult time drinking from a glass without biting it. I bit and broke many glasses in my time. The last glass I remember biting was at age 14 on a cruise ship with my family. Even to this day I am uncomfortable drinking from a fine crystal wine glass. It's not that I want to break it. To the contrary, I am compelled to clench it as hard as I can, hoping not to break it! I have never cut my mouth on the broken glass.

Likewise, I have many motor tics that my mind believes I just have to do one more time... just one more time... but one more time is never enough. I twitch my nose, blink my eyes, curl the big toe on my right foot, focus closely on the cuticle of the index finger of my right hand, and clench my stomach until it hurts, just to name a few. I used to think they were nervous habits and when I tried really hard to control one of them, another one would pop out. That's why I have so many now, but they usually are not all happening at the same time. The neurologist in Virginia drew this information from me and made the clinical diagnosis that I have a form of Obsessive-Compulsive Disorder called Tourette syndrome. That is very interesting because our family doctor diagnosed Tina with OCD when she was a young adult, ten years earlier. I take medication to ease the urges but they never go away entirely. As John became more frustrated with his situation, my headaches and tics became worse.

While writing this book I referenced some journals from ten years ago. One entry really stood out. It was dated Wednesday, April 13, 2005. I wrote:

> *"Maybe I will write my story one day when I'm done working. I should put that into my plan. I'll just start writing and see where it takes me. I'll start with my morning pages. Maybe today will be the start. The middle of the week is nothing special, but the "13th" is a date of interest.*

CHAPTER ONE

> *It's raining outside my sacred window. That's unusual. I like to sit in my sacred room and fixate on the roof next door with the dip in it. Usually the sun shines brightly on that dip in that roof here in Virginia Beach, but this April morning it's gently raining. How did I get here, to this sacred room, in this place in the universe, at this point in time?*

I call it my sacred room because I sit in this space to write my morning pages, to clear scrambled thoughts from my head onto paper. It is "The Artists' Way." If you have read the book by Julia Cameron you will know why I call it sacred. As I sit here, I contemplate all that is going on in my world. John is having a colonoscopy today. Two days ago he had an endoscopy. Blood tests have shown unusual data but nothing significant, thank God! John is my soul mate. We've been together for 20 years. We were both single parents when we met, and helped each other through the trials and tribulations of raising three adolescents. Over the years, John was always there for me. I've come to realize that he is the first and only man I have ever trusted. I can't imagine life without him. I know these tests will be fine.

My work brought me to Virginia Beach two years ago. My career has given John and me numerous opportunities to travel in the United States and Europe, but Canada will always be home. Ontario is where we were born and where we will die (together with any luck). I jumped at this career move for several reasons — another adventure, warmer climate, cultural experience, but most important to me was the idea that John could take a break from work, and fish and golf and reap the rewards of retirement at the young age of fifty, at least for a year or so. That is how long we expected it would take for the US Immigration & Naturalization Service to process our green cards, which would allow John to also work in the USA. It didn't play out that way.

Life should have been a bowl of cherries here. There are museums, shopping, culture, sports, nightclubs, and festivals. But we became soft and complacent at home together. For me it was great. I went out to work each day in a professional environment with interesting projects. For John, it must have been hell. He became a house husband. He did the shopping and cooking, laundry and cleaning, yard work and errands. A glass of wine and dinner in front of the television or out to the restaurant became habit every evening. Despite John's good

> *intentions, it wasn't healthy for either of us. John never pursued any interests of his own. I came to believe he had a mental block that would not let him spend money he wasn't earning. Despite my best intentions, this move was not good for John. Not at all!"*

That was the last entry in my journal until March 2006. John was still anxiously waiting for his green card so that he could get a job in Virginia. Real estate prices had ballooned and were anticipated to burst. We decided to sell our house on Indian River Road for a nice little profit after two years. In December 2005, we rented a little house by the ocean where General Booth Boulevard meets First Street. It was a cute, pastel-yellow cottage and we loved it there. Still, John was bored. The green card application was still in process. We talked often about returning to Canada.

Chapter 29

The 11th Configuration: Family First

Looking back, I have to say that the time I spent at STIHL in Virginia Beach was the highlight of my career. It was not the time that I worked the hardest or contributed the most. It was the time that I felt I had reached the pinnacle and was the most proud of my success. Perhaps I should have stayed there for five years as Karl had requested, but that was not meant to be.

In the spring of 2006, I received a phone call early one morning while still in bed. My son-in-law, JD, announced to me: "Mission complete."

It took me a few minutes to understand that he and Tina were pregnant. I had waited patiently for this day and I was delighted beyond belief.

We had been in Virginia for three years and the green card process was still backlogged to processing 2001 applications. Karl understood the predicament that John was in. When I informed him we were going back to Canada, he convinced me to take a leave of absence in November, before the baby was born, and return to STIHL after Christmas. Perhaps I would decide to stay one more year.

We packed and left Virginia on the US Thanksgiving Day, November 23, 2006, and Bailey D Ross was born on November 27 in Hamilton General Hospital. I lived two hours away in Benmiller, near Lake Huron. In the middle of the night, when I got the phone call that Tina was in labour, I left as soon as I could. Bailey was born before I got there. In fact, she came before the doctors were ready for her. She was a little premature and in distress. Thank God she was strong, and mom and baby were fine in the end.

I stayed with Tina, JD and Bailey at their home in Freelton for the first two weeks to help Tina with the new baby routine. Of course, I wanted to hold Bailey as much as I could and stare at her as long as I could. In time, Tina's OCD and my OCD collided. We can both be stubborn. It was time for me to leave and let their family find their own way. And they did that very well.

Christmas in Benmiller was a joyous occasion. Children make it wonderful. My sister Alison's four children were now age three to thirteen and we had a brand new baby girl. I absolutely love babies. Not one Christmas has passed in our lives without our family being together. Christmas Eve was a special time when Mom was alive. That was usually when we opened presents. Mom would wake me up after midnight and say "Santa was here!" Now we wait for Christmas morning to see what Santa brought. I still feel closest to God on a calm snowy Christmas Eve at home.

As much as we loved our dream home in Benmiller, you can never go back. During the three years we were gone, a lot changed. You can't avoid wear and tear on a house, but you notice the change more when you have been away while it occurred.

After Christmas John agreed that he would look for work in the area, and I would return to Virginia for three months to tie up loose ends at STIHL. We were in our early fifties and could not retire yet. It was John's turn to work while I spent quality time with Tina and Bailey. In the spring of 2007 Tina moved to St. Marys, less than an hour away. Meanwhile, Christine and Don had a second child. Austin was now eight and had a little sister named Brielle. She was two months younger than Bailey and the two cousins would become good friends.

John had trouble finding work because nothing appealed to him. I think it was because he had been out of the work force for too long. It was part depression, part lack of confidence, and part not wanting to do boring, labour-intensive work. John would not even apply to any of the jobs looking for labourers. I pushed him into applying for a road construction job working for a foreman that he had worked for when I met him 20 years earlier. He got the job but he hated it. He complained about it a lot, even more than he complained about NOT having a job in Virginia.

I started to realize that as long as I had known John he had complained about every career job he ever had. I used to think I could find a solution to help him feel content. I helped him get work at FAG Bearings because of the long hot summer hours on road construction. Every change we made after that I thought would somehow make John happier. Not so. I realize now that it is John's nature to complain. He focuses on the negative side of everything from work to politics to money to relationships. In fact, John creates negatives that don't even exist. He sees the glass half empty, I see it half full. I have learned you cannot change another person. You can only change how you react to them. I've been unsuccessful so far. I try not to let John's negativity impact my gratitude in life. I am empathic by nature and therefore am so sensitive to his feelings. But I am proud to say that John never complains about helping a friend and I can always count on him to be there for family and for me.

As I mentioned earlier, I pushed John into accepting a job he didn't want and he came home to a place he was no longer happy in. It wasn't what it used to be. For me, if you are not happy, you do something about it. My cousin Bob was a realtor. He mentioned a Bed & Breakfast home for sale in Stratford. The more I considered it the more appealing it became. We had family and friends in Stratford. There were more work opportunities in Stratford. It was only 20 minutes' drive from Tina in St. Marys. The Stratford Shakespearean Festival was a big draw for tourist B&Bs for a six-month summer season. We would have enough of an income to live on and have winters free to travel. This B&B had an active client list and John would be his own boss. It seemed like a perfect solution to me.

John agreed to look at it. He thought it was alright but was a little hesitant. We had never done this before. We put in a low offer with the contingency that we sold our house in Benmiller. It was accepted. John said, "I'm not selling unless we get the price we want for our house." To our surprise we got it, but John wouldn't sign. We had a fight.

He complained about the job he had, about the house we built, and about the fact that there were no good jobs in the area. I was not going to pass on this opportunity. Finally, I convinced him to agree to sell and move. He did it reluctantly.

Chapter 30

The 12th Configuration: Bed & Breakfast

We moved into Dunn-Drae B&B on Mornington Street in Stratford in September 2007. We had guests the next day. It was really scary and exciting starting this new adventure. The house had eight bedrooms and seven bathrooms. It was a raised bungalow. Our living quarters and the kitchen/dining area were downstairs. The guest rooms were upstairs. I had a fantastic laundry area and pantry. We had a license for four guest rooms but often had all rooms full. We could sleep and feed a maximum of 20 people, including ourselves. In the off season, it was perfect for having parties and family reunions. Christmas Eve 2007 was a good example. We had all our extended family (12 adults, 7 kids and 3 dogs) at one very long dinner table and for a sleepover. Even Santa came and dispensed presents.

John and I developed an assortment of breakfast recipes, themed guest rooms, a website and advertising materials. I built budgets, profit-and-loss spreadsheets and repeat client lists on the computer. The administration part of the business was more time-consuming than the cooking and cleaning part.

We joined the Stratford and Area Bed & Breakfast Association and I volunteered for the executive committee for two years. Running the B&B was a 24/7 commitment throughout the summer. Breakfasts were our favourite part. I did the baking and the fruit while John was the head chef. After breakfast was served we would pour ourselves a cup of coffee and join our guests at the table. That was the fun part. People who travel have such fascinating stories. We got to know many interesting guests from all over the world. There was always lots of laughter, photos and hugs good-bye. Coincidentally, after 50 years, John and I were again playing together in the kitchen, as we had back in kindergarten when we first met quite by accident!

Our hired help, Helen, would arrive and we served her breakfast before she started cleaning the rooms. We cleaned up the kitchen until noon. Then it was laundry time until three, along with baking, grocery shopping, and welcoming new guests from one until four. Of course, nothing stays on schedule. After dinner, I just wanted to rest with no one bothering me. Unfortunately, I couldn't always control that.

John was a very good B&B host although he complained about it most of the time. He would stand in the kitchen looking out the window and say, "I feel like I'm Cinderella and everyone is going to the ball except me." Poor guy! He owned his own business, worked from home, was his own boss, but "I made him do this." He was not happy.

I said to him, "Go out and find a job you'd rather do, and I will run the B&B."

"You can't manage this on your own," he replied. I know that I could have.

A great advantage was that I was able to spend time with Bailey while running the B&B. Whether it was for a few hours in the afternoon or a sleepover in the off season it was a wonderful place for a baby to grow and explore. The kitchen was like a dance floor to scoot around in her walker or ride on the mop that Poppi John pushed around the floor. Bailey took her first steps in February 2008 while we were moving furniture in one of the guest rooms. She named us Gramma and Poppi Duck-Duck because we took her strolling by the Avon River to feed the ducks and swans. I could see that Bailey had a passion for dance from the time she was two years old. She was a choreographer even then when she pretended to be Angelina Ballerina. Now, eight years later, Bailey is in competitive ballet, jazz, musical theatre, and lyrical dance. I can see her passion for choreography. I am living my dance dream through Bailey.

In 2009, I took a work contract with Schaeffler to cover a maternity leave for my friend and former co-worker Tricia. For 14 months I worked flexible hours to coincide with my B&B chores. I still enjoy stepping back into the financial world, temporarily. The extra money came in handy when we took a Mediterranean Cruise with our good friends Jean and John Edmonds.

On January 30, 2011 Tina and JD were blessed with their second daughter, Gracie Jean Maxwell Ross. Again, I missed the birth since I was in the Bahamas at a wedding for Cousin Judy's daughter Amber. Alison was with Tina and assisted the midwife through the birth. I missed it by one day. I thank JD and Tina for the most precious gift — my two beautiful granddaughters.

In April, John and I took Austin and Bailey, our two eldest grandchildren, for a trip to Disney World for four days. The kids were good as gold. Since they were cousins and not siblings they got along very well. Three years later we took all three granddaughters (Brielle, Bailey and Gracie) to Disney World. Tina and JD came as well. The three princesses were treated to carriage rides and royal visits. The parks were extremely busy and chaotic compared to our prior visit. We packed a lot of fun into five days. Tina made us a book of highlights of our once in a lifetime fantasy through the eyes of little girls.

Chapter 31

The 13th Configuration: Retirement

On May 22, 2011, a catastrophic F5 tornado wiped out miles of Joplin, Missouri. The house we owned a decade earlier was in the middle of it. Nothing was left standing, not even a stick. Then on August 21, 2011, an F3 tornado hit Goderich and destroyed a path through Benmiller and the trees directly across the river from our home. We had left there just four years earlier. It all seemed too close for comfort. My son Adam wrote on Facebook, "The forces of nature are trying to wipe out my mother's history." Comments were, "Let me know where she is now so I'll know where not to go."

By this time, John had had enough of the B&B business. He wanted to move. We listed the house and business for sale in 2011, but it did not sell until the middle of 2012, with a closing date of February 2013. I think we would have run the B&B longer if we had offered only two or three rooms. We tried to do too much. In hindsight, we had six successful and interesting years there.

Again, the timing was interesting. In August 2012, Tina somehow acquired West Nile Virus from an infected mosquito. She was extremely ill for a long period of time. The doctors did not correctly diagnose the illness at first and did not know how to treat her symptoms. So, when we sold the

B&B property around the same time, I knew I wanted to move to St. Marys to be near Tina and the girls.

We wanted to downsize in our search for a home. My heart wanted a little stone cottage by the river. St. Marys is famous for its lovely old limestone buildings. Every stone house we looked at needed a lot of work, especially regarding structural beams and basements. We finally settled on a red brick bungalow with a view of the Thames river near the Grand Trunk Trail. It was on the corner of Ontario Street North and Widder Street West. We purchased it before Christmas and moved in on February 6, 2013.

This house is the perfect size for us. We have a gorgeous, peaceful view of the wide, gentle river, lush towering trees, and a church spire in the background. When the sun sets behind the Grand Trunk Railway trestle, the tall stone pillars are painted sunny gold. We have pleasant neighbours our own age in a small community with everything we need. Yet I still have the feeling that one day we will move again, if only for the need for change.

Chapter 32

The Trip of a Lifetime

New Zealand, Australia, Tahiti, Japan

Before we had a closing date for the sale of our B&B, we had planned our trip of a lifetime and were scheduled to leave Canada on February 26, 2013. It turned out to be three weeks after we moved into our new house. February was certainly a busy month.

First class seats, from Toronto to New Zealand, were a comfortable start for a long flight. In Christchurch, we rented a car and toured around the south island, stopping at various B&Bs for a night or two. I kept a journal of the places we stayed and the things we saw. I love New Zealand. It is fresh and green with turquoise glacial lakes and rivers. I would live there as an alternative to Canada.

There were albatrosses, penguins and colonies of seals. We visited the International Antarctic Centre, Fiordland National Park and Kiwi Birdlife Park. Fox Glacier is an area of mountain peaks, impressive glaciers, tranquil lakes, raging rivers, lush rainforests, and a magnificent coastline. This felt like the last unspoiled place on earth.

After two weeks in New Zealand we flew to Melbourne, Australia and picked up a camper van for our four-week tour of Auz. We spent the first three days visiting our friends Mary and Ian at their home near Melbourne, and at their winery at Red Hill. Taking Ian's advice, we headed southwest to the Great Ocean Road which is a world-renowned drive. Bells Beach was preparing for an international surfers' contest. We camped at Kennett River Holiday Park. It is a nature reserve for koalas and birds. A koala we named "Buddy" slept on a branch in a tree above our camper. I loved the smell of eucalyptus trees that filled the park. Large green, red and blue parrots landed on our shoulders looking for nuts or seeds to eat. There were also kookaburras, crimson rosellas and white-crested cockatoos. No dogs were allowed on the reserve for obvious reasons.

Heading back northeast towards Sydney we had some issues with the van's coolant system. The engine kept over-heating and we were afraid of getting stuck in the middle of nowhere. In slow, sporadic jaunts we made it to a Britz dealer to get another travel van.

Next, we stopped in Sydney to visit Sheila and Glen. Sheila is a friend from Canada, and met Glen while vacationing in Auz. They are married and live there now. She hadn't changed a bit, still sweet as ever. She took us on a ferry to the business district at Darling Harbour where the opera house is. By chance, Ellen DeGeneres was filming an outdoor show that day and we were offered free tickets to it. Sheila and I were walking and chatting near the opera house and a young girl tried to interrupt and give us tickets to the "Alan show." We ignored her. Imagine that! We missed a great opportunity because we didn't understand it was "The Ellen Show"! Please forgive me Ellen. Maybe one day I'll get another chance to see you.

Heading north up the Pacific Highway coastal road, we stopped at various campgrounds overnight. Some large Australian farms are 20 million acres, and the owners use a helicopter to round up the cattle. One man can drive a harvester for eight hours and only cover one strip of the crop. There is such an unusual variety of flora and fauna in Auz, and some of the best beaches in the world.

Our Britz GPS stopped working just before we entered Queensland, so we decided to head for the Britz dealer in Brisbane. On the way, we travelled through "Surfer's Paradise" but we were not impressed with the high-rise condos and traffic congestion. It wasn't what I envisioned as a surfer's paradise. I would not go back to Brisbane either. It is too busy and confusing. We wasted three hours trying to find the Britz dealer without a GPS.

North of Brisbane is the Sunshine Coast. This area is sub-tropical and was extremely hot and humid even though it was autumn when we were there. We drove through miles of sugar cane plantations and macadamia nut trees. Then we crossed the Tropic of Capricorn into the tropical climate zone which is even hotter!

Yeppoon, Queensland has the best beach in my opinion. The sand is as soft as baby powder. We stayed at Beachside Caravan Park on the Pacific Ocean. At this inlet, the water was comfortable with gentle waves. I can imagine my grandchildren playing there. It was an undiscovered gem.

On the highway to Mackay I spotted a large kangaroo in the field and two more that were road kill. At the Cooberrie Wildlife Sanctuary there were koalas and kangaroos that we could feed and pet. We met a donkey that loved John and a cockatoo that did not like me. There were emus and peacocks that followed us around, and marmoset monkeys, crocodiles, dingoes, snakes and lizards in cages.

If you are near Mackay, Queensland, I highly recommend staying at Cape Hillsborough Nature Resort. Don't follow your GPS though. Ours took us 14 km down a cow path with pot holes and cows standing on the road. It is not uncommon for kangaroos to roam the campsites. The children in the park learn to look but not touch. Of course, I didn't know that. John took a video of me patting and chatting with a napping kangaroo named "Bridget" near the community showers.

Heading north to the Coral Coast we came to the start of the Great Barrier Reef. We saw mango and banana plantations. This was the entrance to the rainforests and the humidity had increased. We camped at Crystal Cascade Park near Cairns.

The Daintree Rainforest is the oldest continually living rainforest on Earth. It dates back 3.5 billion years according to native experts. Many of the world's medicinal drugs come from plants that live only in this rainforest. We had a terrific native guide for a ten-hour tour. Both the rainforest and the Great Barrier Reef are World Heritage sites. According to astronauts, the Great Barrier Reef can be seen from the moon!

We saw it up close. The highlight of our trip to Australia was snorkeling in the outer reef. The Sea Star set sail at 8 a.m. with 30 guests and six crew. We sped out to snorkel in Michaelmas Cay in the morning. After a buffet lunch, we sailed out 25 miles more, to Hastings Outer Reef. The coral and fish were fabulous. We wore head to toe lycra stinger suits with mitts over the hands so that no skin was exposed. We swam with large sea turtles and saw giant clams open and close. I bopped a couple of jelly fish away from me. I didn't see sharks or barracuda but they were there.

On April 12, we left Australia for 15 hours of travel from Cairns to Brisbane to Auckland, NZ to Papeete in Tahiti. Our destination was The Pearl Resort on the island of Moorea in Tahiti. Before we got on the ferry to Moorea I realized I had lost my travel wallet with my credit card, bank card and health card! It was somewhere between the Auckland airport and the Tahiti airport. The ferry was coming. Think fast. Panic set in.

There was no cash in that wallet because John was holding the cash. I had to alert MasterCard so I needed to buy a phone card. What number do I call? French is the official language of Tahiti. I had to purchase "Pacific francs" currency to buy a phone card from the little shop near the ferry. The French operator could not understand me asking for the MasterCard customer service number. Finally, I got someone to help me get through to MasterCard International in order to cancel my lost card. I made it just in time to get on the ferry. What a horrible way to start the week of our 25th wedding anniversary.

I felt desolate on the ferry, then it started to rain. The heavens were crying for me. There was nothing more I could do at this time. John had a separate credit card for emergencies. My travel wallet was never seen again but fortunately the cards were never used.

At the resort, our garden bungalow had a thatched roof, a big soft bed, fluffy towels, and a private secluded pool outside the patio doors. The smell of fresh tropical flowers was everywhere. The only thing to do was to unpack and have a drink.

I tried paddleboarding for the first time and loved it. A large outer reef blocked the big Pacific waves and created a calm lagoon around the island. The waters were as clear as gin and so many shades of blue, from aqua to navy. It was more beautiful than Hawaii.

After three days, we moved to an over-the-water bungalow, even more special than the garden bungalow. The sitting room had a glass floor revealing the coral and fish swimming below. Off the patio doors was a deck facing the great blue Pacific. From the deck, you could jump into the ocean or watch dolphins swim by. Behind us were palm trees, thatched huts and green, jagged mountain peaks. That was where we spent our 25th anniversary.

We learned that the original natives of Tahiti were happy and healthy. They wore very little clothing and had rather large webbed feet that were perfect for swimming and catching fish. They ate fruit and nuts from the tropical forests. When the missionaries came, the Tahitians were forced to wear shirts and shoes in an effort to socialize them. The shirts caused them to sweat in their hot, humid climate and eventually pneumonia killed the largest portion of their race. Wearing shoes stunted their feet so they became less adept at swimming. Changing their culture did more harm than good.

After seven days we left Tahiti for Osaka, Japan. Adam and his lovely lady Shinobu met us there. Their rented home in Kasai was large by Japanese standards, with big windows. They took us on a bus tour to the small island of Awaji, with a group of Japanese and Indonesian students. It was an amazing opportunity we would not have had without Adam. There were three languages among the 25 of us, and many of us spoke only our native tongue. Yet we played games, sang songs and communicated with expression in a lovely way. We visited beautiful gardens, a party horn factory, and an incense factory and participated in making these items.

Shinobu has a friend named Mim who is a very good cook from Thailand. Mim spent a few days with us as we toured underground bunkers from World War II, the airfield where kamikaze pilots trained for 30 hours before their final mission, and ancient burial grounds from 200 AD.

Adam worked a short distance away in Toyooka and we spent a few days there. My favourite place was the hexagonal rocks that formed when the North and South Poles' magnetism were switched, 1.6 million years ago. They formed amazing artistic curves in the mountainside. Another of my favourite places was the onsens (therapeutic spa baths) that Kinosaki is famous for. Kinosaki is a beautiful tourist village with great food and pubs. I highly recommend the Tajima beef.

On April 26, the four of us took a road trip in Adam's Honda van to the Island of Shikoku. We drove through steep mountainsides and deep villages with pristine rocky rivers. Rice and tea plantations were staggered in tiers on the hillsides. Artistic, ornate clay tile roofs shone in the sun and fascinated me. Love hotels are very popular in Japan. At Shikoku, we stayed at one called Hotel Piano. These rooms are larger and cheaper than regular hotel rooms. They have jet tubs, TV, music, special lighting and large beds. There is no front desk. You select a room from a vending machine showing available rooms. When you are ready to leave, you pay a machine in the room to open the door and let you out.

The next day we headed back to Kasai. John and I had a wonderful trip. We were very grateful for the effort Adam and Shinobu put into entertaining us for our second visit to Japan. I love Shinobu and bless her relationship with Adam. I would love to take Tina and her girls there. Adam is one terrific host and tour guide. On April 29, 2013 we returned to Canada with memories of our trip of a lifetime.

Chapter 33

There's No Place Like Home

I used to be sad when a special trip came to an end. Now I look forward to the familiarity and comforts of home, and the smiles on the faces of my grandchildren. I miss my big comfy chair and my soap operas. I miss my sister and her loving family. But most of all I miss my daughter.

Tina holds a special place in my heart. She is beautiful, intelligent, artistic and strong. That's a good thing because she inherited the "clumsy" gene from my side of the family. When Tina was two years old she could recite the alphabet, count to 20 and print her name. She was an artist before she started kindergarten. Tina was a deep thinker, quiet and reserved as a child. She could have been a dancer or a writer if she chose to. She was considered a "gifted student" in grade school. In high school, she won the Ela Moll award for visual arts. This helped her attain entry to the OCAD. She became a graphic designer and obtained her first career job from networking at a college project awards banquet. Tina has the motivation to overcome any obstacle in her path. She is a perfectionist... and that is a double-edged sword!

I regret not spending more quality time together doing mother/daughter things like spas, shopping trips or lunches. School and work got in the way. From the time Tina went to college we lived in separate cities, often more than two hours apart. Since I retired to St. Marys we have had plenty of opportunities to do those things together. I'm a lucky grandma to live so close to my girls. I think of all three of them as my girls. I should say all four of them. Bessie, their beagle, is my granddog. I love my son-in-law JD like a son. He is very busy as the Canada-wide manager of a Chicago-based company. His job entails a lot of travel and conference calls from home.

In the spring of 2013, Tina was still having severe undiagnosed symptoms from West Nile Encephalitis she had first contracted the year before. At times, it seems to be getting better and then it comes raging back. The doctors don't know enough about it to make a prognosis.

Chapter 34

Tina and West Nile Encephalitis

The timing of Tina's illness coincided with the sale of our Stratford B&B. I believe I was meant to move close to her in St. Marys. Shortly after the sale was official, Tina became ill at the end of August 2012. Her heart raced, she had trouble breathing, numbness and quivering of her left arm, suffered extreme headaches and mental confusion. It looked like she might die and she could not get out of bed. Three times in one week she was taken to London's University Hospital by ambulance. She was tested for meningitis, West Nile virus, Lyme disease and everything else they could think of. She would begin to improve and be sent home until it got worse again. All tests came back negative.

One Saturday in the middle of September, the hospital called her to come in immediately. They indicated that the fluid from a spinal tap that they had taken on her second visit in August, had grown the West Nile virus. Doctors now understand that sometimes the West Nile antibodies take more than two weeks to build up in the blood stream. That's why the previous tests were negative. Had they known that in August when she arrived by ambulance she would have been hospitalized. She could have died from the effects of the virus on her vital organs. So, a follow-up appointment was made with a neurologist in London.

That neurologist told Tina he suspected her symptoms may continue for 18 months with episodes becoming fewer and farther between, but the worst of it should be behind her. Symptoms continued. At her next three-month appointment this same doctor denied she had West Nile virus and suggested treating her for migraines. He clearly did not know how to proceed. University Hospital Emergency records that indicated West Nile virus seemed to disappear. The Perth County Health Unit, which should have been notified, denied that there were any reports of West Nile in Perth County. I was convinced that this was a cover-up conspiracy because someone in the medical field made a mistake with records.

Tina was devastated. She felt she could not live the rest of her life like this. Her symptoms were like mini seizures. In the middle of a conversation she would zone out and not understand words. She lost the ability to control the left side of her body temporarily. In the middle of shopping she could suddenly forget where she was and why she was there. While driving her car she might forget where she was and just park somewhere until she could remember. She would forget what the numbers on a clock meant. You would think Tina looks fine, because often you can't tell how hard she is struggling to focus her mind on each little piece of data that is coming into her brain from her eyes and her ears and other senses.

Everyday things that you and I do without thinking, are a struggle for Tina. For two years, she couldn't get a doctor to understand what was wrong or even admit that something was terribly wrong. Tina was made to feel that she was wasting their time as she constantly tried to find someone who could help. Then there was a breakthrough.

The Perth County Health Unit finally admitted that there were cases of West Nile virus in Perth County in August 2012. They called Tina and advised her not to donate blood, ever. Further tests were done and an MRI of the brain showed an area in the right frontal lobe that had dried blood from a brain insult, likely encephalitis, which is a swelling of the brain.

From my understanding, what happened to Tina rarely happens with West Nile. She was bitten by an infected mosquito. The virus was in her bloodstream and happened to get into her spinal fluid. From there it went to her brain and caused swelling. That was the end of August when she was deathly sick and symptoms were mostly on the left side of her body. Tina was strong enough to survive that. The swelling went down but the brain insult is still there. That area of her brain can only handle limited amounts of data at a time. When she is at home and life is calm, her brain can receive and transmit limited amounts of data. When there is a high volume of data streaming in, her brain shuts down certain functions that it cannot handle. For example, in a grocery store with many items on many shelves, she may only be able to recognize one item at a time and have trouble finding the item she is looking for. In the hair salon with many mirrors and lights and noises, her stylist noticed she seemed to become catatonic. Our brains transmit thousands of messages automatically, like when you are driving and pause at a traffic light. Your brain controls your breathing, your heart beating blood through your veins, tells you to check the colour of the light, reminds you to see if there are people in the crosswalk, you want to turn left, your ears tell your brain you hear music on the radio, and you may be thinking about being late for work. This is multitasking at extremes. Tina's brain cannot handle all that data.

There is no cure for this as far as we know. It's been four years now and Tina is learning techniques to improve her life. Most importantly she knows what she needs to avoid. To this day, she cannot watch a 3-D movie. A trip to Disney World was a family adventure that drained her. I applaud her endurance for the sake of her children. I am so proud of Tina and JD weathering this storm in their life while nurturing two little girls. This too shall pass.

Chapter 35

Life's a Struggle, As It Should Be

The German philosopher Friedrich Nietzsche was wise when he stated: "That which does not kill us makes us stronger." I have found strength in those words most of my life, and tried to implant them in my children. Everyone struggles through life.

Changing schools, leaving friends behind, feeling different and alone — these were all hardships that I accepted growing up. As an adult, I resented the fact that I hadn't formed long term relationships as others had. I developed the habit of constantly reconfiguring my persona based on my intuition of what was expected of me by the people around me at the time. It happened automatically. Avoidance of conflict was part of it. A desire to please and be accepted into the pack was another reason.

The car crash of 1966 had a negative impact on my life forever, or so I thought. But I will never know how different my life would have been had it not happened. I would have taken different paths, had different friends, and different struggles. For all I know my life could have been worse.

From those struggles I learned that gratitude and kindness are the secret to happiness. If you FEEL grateful for what you have, no matter how little, you ARE happy by default. If you are kind to others, regardless of their attitude, you feel light and sunny. Everyone is struggling with something, and just a kind word or a smile will lift their spirits and warm yours. It's easy to be kind to nice people. It's harder to be kind to mean people, but the payoff is much higher.

I believe my struggles were all part of God's plan for me. Some call it fate or coincidence. Life unfolds in surprising ways. It's tempting to blame God for adversity. I have come to learn that struggles require effort and change, and lead to new possibilities and opportunities we would ignore if we were content. Contentment leads to boredom and lethargy. I'm not saying contentment is bad. Just beware that it can make you soft. Motivation comes from discontent. A fulfilling life requires purpose, compromise, challenge and change.

It is ironic that for most of my working life I looked forward to retirement and peace of mind. Now that I'm here, it's not as great as I had anticipated. It's all about the journey, not the destination. Joy comes from achievement over struggles, motivation to face challenges, and the gift of giving. I didn't recognize this sage advice when I was growing up and going through it. It's so clear now in the rear-view mirror.

In 2011, I found a new outlet to maintain my sanity. Many thanks to the creative minds of Ev Scott and her daughter Jaime Martin. They created a women's group called W.I.N.G.S. (Women In Netweaving Groups Soar). Joining W.I.N.G.S. has led to friendships with very like-minded, lovable ladies who are supportive, artistic, and passionate about life.

The other thing that keeps me sane and brings love and laughter to my life, is of course my girls — Tina, Bailey and Gracie. They call me the Adventure Gramma. We have been to Disney World, Mexico, summer cottages at the lake, pony riding, elephant riding, dancing, and theatre. Yes, life is a struggle. Find someone to share it with.

Postscript

I would like to thank everyone who has at one time or another walked through life with me, especially those who I have included in this book. I acknowledge that some may remember things differently, but I have been as honest and factual as my memory and perception can be. I sincerely hope I have not offended anyone as that was never my intention.

Looking back, I see the incidental events that shaped my personality. I am an introvert who wears the mask of an extravert. No one knows the little girl who still lives inside of me. The one who hates conflict, needs to be accepted, and is afraid to say, "No thank you." Six decades later I am getting to know her. Writing this book has helped a great deal.

I have always had recurring night dreams. In my teens, I dreamt about the house on Langley Street where I had been most happy. In one dream, there was a duck and a cow in my driveway. They were fighting violently. I couldn't get past them to go in the house. The duck was vicious. It bit the cow's leg off. I panicked for the poor cow. Someone help the cow! This was a recurring nightmare.

Around the time my mom passed away I started dreaming that I could fly like a bird. It felt so real. I had that dream thousands of times. I still have that dream but often now it starts with climbing on rocks and cliffs and I can jump down from great heights and gently land on my feet.

In other recurring dreams, I cannot get to where I'm going. Sometimes I'm in school and cannot find my locker, I cannot find my classroom, and I cannot find my way home. Sometimes I'm on a ship or in a grand hotel and I cannot find my room, the room numbers are not in sequence. I am going from floor to floor, I cannot find my key. I'm always lost in familiar places. The same locations occur in dream after dream as if I have been there before.

My most frequent disturbing dream is trying to find Mom. I am in Stratford. She is living in an upper apartment. I am walking and the streets are familiar but I can't get to her street. I try to phone her but can't remember her number. I get the operator but the key pad won't work. I can't hit the right numbers on the key pad. Sometimes, I find the street but the stairs are upside down. I can't get to her door. I can never fly in this dream. I can never reach her.

I have no idea what all of this means, but I can speculate. I went many places and touched many lives but I wasn't able to make lasting connections. In my dreams, I am lost in a big world. Now I am happiest at home with my family, until the last configuration, when I become a butterfly.

Chronology

Year	Age	Address	Event
1953	Born	RR4 Stratford	
1958	5		Kindergarten – Juliette School
1959	6		Grade 1 – Romeo School
1959	6 ½		Grade 1 – Juliette School
1960	7		Grade 2 – Country school house
1960	7 ½		Grade 2 – Hamlet School
1961	8	334 Douglas St, Stratford	Grade 3 – Avon School
1962	9	20B Almond Rd, London	Mother married Ralph Bailey Grade 4 – C.C.Carruthers School
1963	10		Grade 5 – Glen Cairn School
1964	11	Westminster Apt, London	Grade 6 – Princess Elizabeth School Sister Alison was born
1965	12	214 Langley St, London	Grade 7 to 8 – Tecumseh School
1966	13		June 11 – Car crash

1967	14		Grade 9 to 10 – South Collegiate, London Part-time work – Hospital patient feeder – Magazine sales
1969	16	204 Front St, Stratford	Grade 11&12 – Stratford Central Secondary Part-time work – Stratford Hospital kitchen
1971	18	Albert St Apt, Stratford	Married; Work – International Artcraft
1972	19	Caledonia St	Tina was born; Bought first house Several part-time jobs
1974	21		Adam was born; Direct selling
1975	22	Huron Road, Sebringville	Moved to a three-bedroom house
1977	24		Store manager – Kwikie Minit Market
1978	25		Timekeeper - Canadian Fabricated Prod.
1980	27	Downie St Apt, Stratford Back to Sebringville	Moved out with children for three months Waitress - English Parlour Inn
1981	28		Accounts receivable - Blackstone Ind.
1982	29	Campbell Crt, Stratford	Moved out with children final time Laid off at Blackstone Became a dog groomer
1983	30	649 Devon St, Stratford	Accounts payable - American Motors
1984	31		Met John Lyoness
1985	32		Enrolled with Society of Management Acct. Divorce Granted
1986	33	244 Church St, Stratford	John and I combine families.
1988	35		Marriage to John Lyoness
1989	36		Christine moved to her mother's Adam moved to his father's

1990	37	Huron Rd, Shakespeare	Downsized our home
1991	38		Tina goes to college in Toronto
1992	39	Stratford	Cost Accountant - FAG Bearings Ltd, Stfd.
1995	42		Graduated CMA (now CPA, CMA)
1996	43	Joplin, Missouri, USA	Promotion to controller, FAG USA
1999	46	Athlone Cres, Stratford	FAG Canada, special projects manager
2000	47	Benmiller Line, Clinton	Built our dream home on the Maitland River
2003	50	Virginia Beach, VA, USA	move to STIHL Inc; Finance project mgr.
2006	53	Benmiller Line, Clinton	November – Return home; Bailey is born
2007	54	278 Mornington St, Stfd.	Purchase Dunn-Drae B&B
2009	56		14-month contract; Schaeffler (FAG)
2011	58		Granddaughter Gracie is born
2012	59		Tina contracted West Nile Virus
2013	60	110 Ontario St N, St. Marys	Sold B&B; Retired; Trip to South Pacific

About the Author

I often wished my mother had written a book about her life. She told me so many fascinating stories about growing up poor in the 1930s and 1940s in rural Perth County, Ontario, Canada. Now that she has been gone more than 20 years I struggle to recall them. Yet they are important to me.

Recently I had lunch with my friend, Tricia. After a few chuckles about recent events she declared that I should write a book about my life. I had heard that comment before but this time it sparked in my brain and continued to sizzle for months. I couldn't erase it, and because of my mother's unrecorded history, I felt I needed to record my own story for my granddaughters.

I had the title before I started to write the story. The number 13 is a recurring phenomenon in my life. I started a new school as many times and each time I reinvented myself. At age 13 my life changed drastically. In 2013, I began writing this book. The major events in my life seemed to be guided by a force with a purpose. I am empathic and intuitive. There are dimensions in this universe we don't understand as yet. I can sense them. My daughter laughs at me when I talk like this. She says I'm just on a different wavelength!

CPSIA information can be obtained
at www.ICGtesting.com
Printed in the USA
LVOW07s0042060118
562042LV00001BA/6/P

9 781773 701615